Essays at the End of the Age

Essays at the End of the Age

The Death of Nihilism and the Rebirth of Truth and Beauty

JAY TROTT

Wipf & Stock
PUBLISHERS
Eugene, Oregon

ESSAYS AT THE END OF THE AGE
The Death of Nihilism and the Rebirth of Truth and Beauty

ISBN 10: 1-55635-057-0
ISBN 13: 978-1-55635-057-3

Manufactured in the U.S.A.

Contents

End Game

THE FIRST time it jumped out at us was in the *Inquiry Concerning Human Understanding*, where Hume goes out of his way to make himself sound friendly to observational science in order to neutralize his readers' Newtonian defenses.

What's strange about this is that Hume was a radical Rationalist, an advocate of the power of the mind to make its own happiness and eschew any slavery to science and its limited concepts of value. He was the chief of skeptics when it came to empiricism of the Newtonian type because he was opposed to its determinism. Newton's universe runs like a finely-tuned clock; there is no wiggle room for idealists to try to create something better. Hume wanted to overturn this determinism through pure intellect and its capacity to cast doubt on any valuation that involves a construct of intellect and sense. It was too late for a revival of Idealism in the pure sense, however, with its open contempt for empirical science—the enthusiasm for Newton was simply too strong. So he adopted a subtle strategy for overthrowing his foes. Instead of openly condemning empirical science, he made a feint toward Newton while attempting to roll up the left flank of the enemy.

Hume's feinting strategy was designed to afford him an advantage on the battlefield of philosophy. The premise of philosophy is that it is possible to obtain happiness through intellect and its qualitative power, its capacity to judge what is "good," but the philosophers were divided from the beginning between those who thought that the good of happiness was pure intellect and those who tried to describe it as some sort of construct of intellect and sense. The conflict between these two schools cannot be resolved because intellect with its qualitative force of resistance is not the same thing as sense. Plato's ideal of pure intellect leads to dualism—to nothingness—by negating all existent values. Aristotle tried to overcome this problem by describing the good as a synthesis of intellectual and material causes, but sense and intellect cannot be mixed in any degree without depriving intellect of the purity of its resistance and the highly desirable freedom it intimates from the determined conditions of existence.

This divide between intellect and sense came about through the eagerness of the philosophers to equate intellect with the good—to make intellect the essence of God, or transcendent being. The goodness of intellect is found in its capacity for judgment—the qualitative force of resistance that enables it to determine what is "good"—but this force of resistance cannot be totalized as a transcendent value without dividing it from sense. There is goodness in intellect for its own sake, and there is also great value in nature, but it is impossible to overcome the difference between intellect and existent values. Neither Plato nor Aristotle can obtain a clear-cut victory on the battlefield of philosophy because neither one can furnish an undivided description of the good.

This problem was not clear to medieval Europe when Greek philosophy was rediscovered after the Crusades. At that time the battle between the philosophers seemed fairly straightforward. Thomas Aquinas was quite open about which school he belonged to and where his allegiance lay because he had confidence in the power of his arguments to carry the day—and the same was true of Pico and Ficino. But over time it became clear that the war could not be won by straightforward means. The Schoolmen and Renaissance Neoplatonists were divided in the same way as Plato and Aristotle. Both sides were able to provide plausible arguments for their concepts of "the good," but those arguments were divided by the nature of intellect itself and led to unsatisfactory results.

Descartes was the first to try to change this dynamic by pretending to be something other than what he really was—or perhaps it would be more accurate to say that he believed the cogito was something new when in fact it had the same limitations as Idealism. Like Plato, Descartes was a lover of pure intellect and its capacity to render clear and simple value judgments. He had a strong aversion to the convoluted value judgments produced by Scholasticism, which were based on the notion that sense objects are a ratio of intellectual and material causes. Scholasticism could lead to risibly ornate descriptions of nature that were also sometimes blatantly false, as became evident when Galileo ran afoul of the metaphysical science establishment for reporting what he had observed about the motions of the planets.

Those great discoveries inspired Descartes to describe what he believed to be a new kind of science, not based on metaphysics but on the combined power of direct observation and pure mind. He did not think of himself as a follower of Plato because Plato had dismissed observational science as mere materialism. Descartes was a Christian who believed that the universe had been created by God and was good. He accepted the basic premise of Scholasticism that the eternal qualities of God are seen in everything that has been made. But he also believed that pure intellect had the power to purge science of the metaphysical accretions it had accumulated through Scholasticism. Since he agreed with the philosophers that intellect was the essence of God, it seemed to him that it was possible to obtain a crystal-clear picture of nature as well as of the will of transcendent being by using pure intellect to analyze the sensuous universe God had made.

But Descartes did not realize that it is impossible to read the goodness of intellect into nature without some sort of construct of intellect and sense. The value judgments formed by intellect on the basis of what it observes in nature are not found in the things themselves and in fact are quite different from those things. Thus the strict resistance of the cogito to constructs of value did not lead to the knowledge of transcendent being predicted by Descartes. It led instead to the purely observational science of the 18th century, from which all metaphysical speculation had been meticulously purged; it led to the concept of the great chain of being, confirming Aquinas's complaint that methods rooted in pure intellect produce "nothing but metaphors." Descartes did not share Plato's snobbish abhorrence of observational science, but the cogito led to the same nothingness as Idealism in the end by negating the possibility of using nature for philosophical purposes. It drew a bright line between observational science and philosophy and its pursuit of the good—not at all what Descartes intended.

At least Descartes did not feign his interest in observational science. He seems to have genuinely believed that it was possible to apply his love of pure intellect to science in order to obtain value judgments about the good. His method was too young for him to be aware of the fact that it is impossible to overcome the age-old divide between intellect and sense through the cogito, which reflected a love of pure intellect. This was no longer true by the time of Hume, however. Newton's response to the cogito (and Locke's) was so successful that it was no longer possible for lovers of pure intellect to harbor any illusions about their ability to overcome their foes by straightforward means. This difficulty gave birth to the feinting strategy that became prevalent in the modern age. Hume made himself *sound* like a lover of observational science—but only to appropriate some of the rhetorical resources of his foes and throw them back on their heels.

Putting on the rhetoric of the enemy is not the same thing as conceding his point; and in fact Hume's feint demonstrates that it is quite possible to make oneself sound like a committed empiricist while also clinging fervently to pure intellect, even though these two values are diametrically opposed. His argument about the unpredictability of physics cannot be reconciled to cause-and-effect descriptions of nature by any means. Indeed, it is a blunt attack on observational science and its capacity to draw philosophical conclusions on the basis of cause. Hume was tapping into the disgust with Christianity that came in the wake of the Reformation and its religious wars. He wanted to shake the faith of the herd in Newton's seemingly invincible God and raise them up on the wings of a new philosophy guided by reason alone and unencumbered by theology or teleology. But Newton was too strong to be attacked by conventional means. His forces were entrenched. Hence the only way to obtain an advantage on the battlefield was to use a feinting strategy.

Hume's feint set the tone for modern philosophy and its increasingly elaborate rhetorical strategies for outflanking the enemy. An immediate response came in the form of the Transcendental Aesthetic. There were two things about Hume that bothered Kant. In his eagerness to glorify Rationalism, Hume appeared to dismiss observational science. His argument had the effect of setting philosophy apart from science, as if science were beneath philosophers and had nothing of importance to say about truth or value. But his antipathy to Newton's God also had a more far-reaching effect: it removed God from philosophy. Hume was an advocate of the ability of philosophers to point the way to happiness by their own inner light; by human reason for its own sake, without invoking God. This was troubling to Kant, who foresaw that taking God out of philosophy would negate the possibility of making value judgments about what is good—would result in the annihilation of philosophy itself and its pursuit of "the good" of happiness.

Hence the strategic goals of Kant's response to Hume (and indirectly to the cogito) were twofold: to restore the transcendent to philosophy, and to reassert the utility of observational science to making value judgments about what is good. This twofold strategy translated into the first of the great offensive-defensive phrases of the modern era—the Transcendental Aesthetic. The feinting power of this phrase comes from the fact that the first word does not mean what it seems to say. Kant was a follower of Aristotle, not Plato. He believed that value judgments about what is good should be rooted in existent values; but existent values are not transcendent. Indeed, the main limitation of synthetic methods is that they must forfeit the transcendent resonance of "the good" in order to describe it as an immanent value. Aristotle did not supersede Plato with his construct of value because Plato continued to appeal to those who desired the seeming purity of Idealism and its power to intimate transcendent values.

Kant was a follower of Aristotle and his constructive method—but he was able to make himself *sound* like an Idealist by beginning his famous phrase with the word "transcendental." In spite of its appearance, this word has nothing to do with transcendent values. The Transcendental Aesthetic is firmly rooted in existent values but is said to obtain "transcendental" significance through certain fixed realities in consciousness that inform our value judgments about nature—such as time and space. Later on Kant made a sharp distinction between transcendent values and transcendental valuations; but by then the psychological impression had already been created. He had succeeded in making himself sound like an Idealist.

Methods of obtaining the good of happiness that are rooted in pure intellect lead to nothingness because pure intellect is the same thing as pure resistance to the unhappiness of existence. Synthetic philosophers attempted to overcome this problem by grounding their concepts of what is good in the goodness of existent values. Aristotle and Plato both believed that the good was intellect; the difference was that Plato linked the good to pure resistance to embodied values while Aristotle attempted to define it as a synthesis of intellectual and material causes. But just as Plato could not equate the good with pure intellect without negating existent values, so Aristotle could not describe it as a construct of intellect and matter without depriving intellect of some of its goodness—of its qualitative force of resistance, which is the very thing that makes it different from matter.

Aristotle wanted to have it both ways. He wanted to equate intellect and its capacity for resistance with the good, but he also wanted to make a case for the concept that the desire for knowledge of the good can be satisfied through observation of existent values. Kant was a follower of Aristotle in the sense that he claimed to be able to overcome the nothingness caused by the cogito by rooting his value judgments in the goodness of existent values. He wanted to retain the purifying power of the cogito, which intimates transcendent value, but at the same time he did not want to let go of Newtonian science and its seeming power to identify transcendent influences in nature. The word *transcendental* is used to reassure readers that he has not abandoned the cogito and its purifying power, while *aesthetic* conveys the impression that his philosophy has the power to go beyond Rationalism and produce substantive value judgments about what is good.

Just as Hume's feinting strategy caused him to become identified as an empiricist in spite of the fact that he dismissed the value of observational science to philosophy, so Kant's rhetorical strategy was so effective that he became known as the father of "German Idealism" when in reality he was a follower of Aristotle and repeatedly cited him in his descriptions of his method. He used the term "transcendental idealism" to describe the full scope of his method—philosophy as well as aesthetics—but he was not an Idealist in any sense of the word beyond having a theory about the nature of ideas. Indeed, the purpose of his philosophy was to "annihilate" the self-existent idea as invoked by Descartes and crown the synthetic method as the final resolution of the problems found in philosophy. And the power of his feinting strategy was such that even Emerson, who identified himself as a follower of Plato, also considered himself a Transcendentalist.

The Transcendental Aesthetic was the first of many ingenious two-word offensive-defensive feints in modern philosophy, such as "dialectical materialism," which is neither dialectical in the Hegelian sense nor materialism in the strict sense of pure matter without spiritual content. The most potent of all such phrases, however, was "natural selection." Darwin was a philosopher in addition to being a scientist, and as a philosopher he was a new type of idealist. He did not believe in God or the good, like Plato, or in self-existent ideas, but he shared Plato's love of the unifying power of ideas and theory, and he believed that the unifying value of natural selection was leading to a transcendent form of existence. Nature was not merely evolving but rising and becoming more "fit"—which in Darwin's mind meant more beautiful and valuable; more civilized.

In short, Darwin was not an Idealist in the traditional sense, but he was highly idealistic about evolution, which he assumed to be an ameliorative power that was somehow beautifying existence. It was this belief in the transcendent potential of evolution that enabled him to go far beyond the realm of pure science and capture the popular imagination. Darwin's description of evolution leaves the impression that it is possible for humanity to find the happiness it desires through purely natural processes, without the help of a meddlesome God. The simplicity of this notion seemed especially appealing at the time because of Hegel and his attempt to synthesize being and nothingness, which led to such abstruse results that Transcendentalism had become a burden to the human spirit.

Darwin exploited this discontent by making it seem that the transcendent being was superfluous to the pursuit of happiness. He raised the stakes on the appropriation strategy to a new level by making himself out to be a paragon of observational science when in fact he was an idealist and lover of theory. Hume had merely *talked* about his enthusiasm for empiricism; Darwin went far beyond him by telling a story in which he appeared to have actually lived it, describing himself as a naïve believer who set out on his voyage of discovery with no preconceptions at all about the matter of origins. By this account, he did not arrive at the theory of evolution until he had been overwhelmed by the facts and could not reasonably have come to any other conclusion. But of course Darwin was an enthusiastic reader of Lemark and Lyell and could hardly have been unaware of the celebrity of his own grandfather.

Darwin also made effective use of rhetorical feinting strategies. The phrase "natural selection" is clever on many levels. To begin with, the word *natural* is a feint to Kant and Transcendentalism. Kant responded to the nothingness caused by Rationalism by indicating that knowledge of transcendent value can be obtained through the sensuous values that already exist, much as Aristotle had claimed that the nature of the good can be found in the goodness of nature. It is the goodness of nature that gives Transcendentalism its power to win the hearts and minds of men and forms the ideological core of Romanticism. Darwin's use of "natural" as his lead word, then, constituted a feint toward Transcendentalism and was a clever way of appropriating its rhetorical power, just as Kant had used the word "transcendental" to neutralize Descartes.

But the most ingenious part of the offensive-defensive phrase, as has often been pointed out, is the word *selection*, which implies some sort of mechanism in nature which is capable of producing amelioration. The term "natural selection" casts a spell over the mind by making men believe they are on a mysterious journey that leads to the happiness of transcendent fitness; that all of their trials and tribulations will pass away in time because nature is already in the process of selecting the most beautiful and fit to survive; that they themselves are in fact in some strange way selected—nature's elect. In reality, however, nature cannot be said to select anything at all. Nature is not a discretionary power. It has no innate knowledge of what is valuable and cannot be made to stand in for God. Darwin was aware of this problem, which is why he proposed "survival of the fittest" as an alternative; but he neglected to renounce natural selection and its transcendent resonance. He found a way to make it seem that he preferred the scientific phrase while not actually letting go of the philosophical one; and this clever sleight of hand was the key to his success, since it was the glittering notion of natural selection that caught the popular imagination, not the survival of the fittest, which sounds rather grim.

Natural Selection enabled Darwin to outflank the Transcendentalists by substituting nature for transcendent being, but this clever maneuver also signaled the end of the feinting game and of philosophy itself. Philosophy is based on the pursuit of happiness—"the good," the highest desire of humankind. This blissful state cannot be found in human existence, but the philosophers justified their methods of describing it by attributing it to a transcendent being. If there is no such being—as Darwinism indicates—then the good of happiness does not exist. And without the promise of happiness, philosophy loses its power over the imagination.

Apparently this problem was not clear to Nietzsche when he proposed Nihilism as the antidote to Transcendentalism. Nietzsche was an ardent admirer of Darwin and the concept that it is possible to obtain transcendence by negating God and embracing the unifying principle in nature indicated by the survival of the fittest, which he called the will to power. Those who embraced this principle would go beyond the mixed state of being seen in Hegel's "superior man" and become supermen. Nietzsche claimed that it was possible to obtain this state of purity by negating any concept of "being" in favor of pure nothingness. Since the word "being" reflects transcendent being, his theory required the negation of God, or the good. But the purity obtained through Nihilism also doomed philosophy, which has no reason to exist without the good of happiness.

Nietzsche was merely the messenger, however. The good had been "dead" to philosophy for some time. Philosophy cannot overcome the dividedness seen in its descriptions of the good because intellect and its concepts of value are divided by the difference between itself and sense. The feinting strategy seen in the modern era represented an attempt to go beyond the stalemate that had prevailed since Plato and Aristotle, but it was self-limiting. It could not sustain itself once the Idealists had succeeded in making themselves out to be empiricists and lovers of constructive methods had convinced us that they were Idealists. At that point, the feinting potential of the strategy was exhausted, and philosophy lost its seeming forward motion.

The strategy of appropriation produced a temporary advantage on the battlefield in modern philosophy, but it could not overcome the difference between intellect and sense. The modern era, with its elaborate rhetorical strategies, was an endgame, and it led to the annihilation of philosophy in the end.

Revolution

S INCE MARX, revolution, sudden change, has generally been attributed to radicals and lovers of absolutes and their resistance to constructs of value. But what if revolution were a potentiation of the paradigm? What if revolution were more naturally akin to the imposition of a new construct of value than to absolutism?

In Hegel's paradigm of history, a new and higher construct of being is said to have been evolving over the ages through the conflict of thesis and antithesis. The antithesis may seem sudden and abrupt, since it is the negation of an existing construct of value, while the synthesis is constructive and thus appears to involve a more gradual process. But in reality the antithesis may be the more gradual agent. Constructs of value can be progressively undone for the very reason that they *are* constructs—they are quantitative and can be incrementally reduced. Absolute values, on the other hand, cannot be progressively undone. They must be overthrown by the imposition of a new construct of value.

The antithesis reflects the fact that human beings are in a state of permanent resistance to the unhappiness of existence. The fountainhead of antithetical methods is Idealism—and it is interesting to note that Plato's description of how to obtain happiness was distinctly gradualistic. Plato found himself confronted with an array of value judgments about the good that were rooted in sense and did not seem to get to the essence of things. In his view, the good was pure intellect; the things we perceive with our senses were considered to be nothing more than shadows of the good and the forms of value it imposes on existence. Thus it seemed to him that it was possible to ascend the steps of wisdom by progressively negating any valuation that involved a construct of intellect and sense.

Plato's steps for ascending to the throne of the highest good are just that—they are steps. In other words, they are gradual in nature. And this same gradualism can also be seen in Descartes, the modern paragon of the antithesis, and his resistance to Scholasticism. The Schoolmen had produced an elaborate construct of being that was cumbersome and sometimes seemed wildly unconnected to reality. Descartes claimed to be able to cut through this jungle of metaphysics through pure intellect and obtain scientific judgments that were perfectly clear and comprehensible. Very much like Plato, the process he described was gradual: each scientific proposition was to be assessed individually and accepted or rejected on its merits.

The gradual nature of absolutism can be seen in the analogy of property rights, which can be thought of as a political correlative of the synthetic method. Property rights provide an innate force of resistance to absolutism; land ownership forms a natural construct in the sense that land itself is quantifiable and limited. Just as land is a concrete entity that can be decreased incrementally, so property rights can be diminished gradually through taxation and social legislation or other means on the road to absolutism. But the absolutism seen, for instance, in Plato's *Republic*, cannot be changed progressively because it is a totality. The only way to undo it is to overturn it by force.

The Romantic age was a revolutionary era. Philosophy changed radically with the imposition of Kant's construct of intellect and sense. The purpose of the construct was to overthrow Rationalism and the nothingness that resulted from the doubting power of the cogito by describing a middle ground between Rationalism and Empiricism. Rationalism as seen in someone like Hume was an absolute value—totalized doubt; pure skepticism. It could not produce any substantive judgments because it was rooted in the capacity of intellect to resist all constructs of value. Nor can pure skepticism be diminished by incremental means. It can only be overthrown through a new construct of value.

The imposition of Kant's construct coincided with political revolutions that marked the end of the age of the absolute rulers. The American Colonies consisted mostly of landowners; when they felt their natural rights imperiled, they rose up against the king and enshrined their love of independence in a construct of checks and balances. Initially their polity depended upon Locke, but the impact of Transcendentalism can also be seen in Jefferson and agrarian democracy. Jefferson's concept of a nation governed by gentleman planters was linked to the revolutionary spirit of the age through the Transcendental Aesthetic, which was based on Aristotle and his belief in the goodness of nature. Aristotle resisted the nothingness of Idealism by claiming that the good can be discerned in nature as a ratio of intellectual and material causes, a concept of the good that tends to glorify nature. It also tends to favor private property as a check on oligarchy and despotism, which Aristotle regarded as the meanest forms of government.

Aristotle favored democracy and freedom but tempered this freedom by rooting democratic rule in a golden mean—in a large middle class, which is not too rich for its own good or too poor to look beyond the immediate needs of the body. This middle class was not the bourgeoisie of modern capitalism but the propertied class of an agricultural society that obtained its wealth through husbandry. Aristotle considered it suitable substance for democracy because it rose through natural means—through farming, which connected it to the goodness of nature. And this same belief in the goodness of nature and the wisdom obtained through husbandry is also the basis of Jeffersonian democracy.

Aristotle and Jefferson were both constructionists, both democrats—but neither one was a political gradualist. Just as Aristotle devoted a chapter of his book on politics to revolution and the occasional need to overthrow despots in order to impose a democratic construct, so Jefferson considered himself a revolutionary figure and opposed the tyrants of his age. This suggests that the constructive method may be naturally revolutionary; that it derives some of its impetus from a need to overthrow the tyranny of absolutism, whether in politics or philosophy.

By contrast, Marxism *sounded* revolutionary but turned out to be gradualistic in its effects. Marx believed that capitalism would reach a tipping point and be overturned in a moment of crisis; but capitalism is a construct, and as such it is capable of incremental change. Marx wrote at a time when industrial capitalism was experiencing growing pains. The oppressive working conditions seen in factories and coal mines made it seem despotic, and he believed those abuses would lead to a hardening of class lines and revolution. This hardening never materialized, however. The worst abuses were already being addressed in Marx's time. Meanwhile the middle term of supply and demand was driven down in search of larger markets, making commodities available to a wider range of consumers. "Dialectical materialism" did not prevail in capitalist countries because industrial capitalism proved to be the ultimate satisfier of material needs. In countries where Marx-inspired revolutions did occur, one form of totalitarianism was simply replaced with another—Bolshevism for the Czar, for example.

And yet there has been a *gradual* trend in capitalist countries toward the very thing Marx desired. The possibility of gradualism is inherent in capitalism, which is a construct of property as well as supply and demand. Property rights were eroded through social legislation in favor of absolute rights. A democratic form of socialism came into being which proved to be increasingly tyrannical. It stifled individual initiative by removing economic incentive and favoring collectivism. It created new types of oligarchies by emphasizing absolute and collective rights over property rights. It spawned sprawling bureaucracies that leached on the lifeblood of the state. These changes happened gradually and incrementally as the construct of value that is capitalism gave way to socialism—but they cannot be reversed incrementally because socialism is totalitarian value. The unraveling of modern socialism is not gradual but revolutionary in nature.

The same progressive trend toward absolutism is also evident in modern culture. Modernism is the antithesis of Transcendentalism. Kant used the Transcendental Aesthetic to overthrow the radical doubt that developed through Rationalism and its resistance to constructs of value. This doubt leads to nothingness by making it impossible to arrive at any positive concept of value. Kant thought he could overcome this nothingness by describing a construct of Rationalism and the concepts of being seen in Empiricism. He claimed it was possible to obtain "transcendental" valuations by discerning the influence of transcendent forces on human thinking; but in order to arrive at such valuations, it was necessary to set aside the transcendent and its force of resistance. If the transcendent is pure intellect, as the philosophers believed, then it must be set aside in order to arrive at any substantive value judgment, because pure intellect is the same thing as pure negation.

Setting aside the transcendent force of resistance provided by the cogito is not gradualism; it is revolution. Kant overthrew Rationalism through the construct of value that he called the "transcendental aesthetic"—but there was a fatal flaw in this construct. As soon as synthetic philosophers agreed to set aside the transcendent, they lost the justification for their method of judging value. Kant tried to circumvent the teleology of Scholasticism by indicating that he was seeking transcendental valuations in the human mind for its own sake. Unlike Aristotle and Thomas Aquinas, he did not directly invoke a Transcendent Being to justify his method of judging value; instead he claimed to be looking for the footprint of transcendent forces in the way that humans think about being. But by setting aside the transcendent, Kant forfeited the ability to claim that Transcendentalism has the power to provide any insight into transcendent value. The supernal influences he thought he saw in human thinking may be nothing more than a delusion.

The reaction to Transcendentalism was revolutionary in *tone*. Nietzsche did not describe gradual steps for liberating the superman from the bondage of Kant's construct of value; instead he attempted to annihilate that construct by declaring "God is dead." If the transcendent being does not exist, then Transcendentalism is quite literally nothing and appears to collapse like a house of cards. But Nihilism was the antithesis of a construct of value, and its actual effects were gradual, not revolutionary. The Modernists used the power of nothingness to question all constructs of being, a process that is still ongoing in Deconstruction and Postmodernism. If Hegel was right that any concept of being is already a synthesis of being and nothingness, then Nihilism can be used in a progressive fashion to negate those constructs until there is nothing left but nothingness.

This is just what has happened in the modern age. All value judgments that indicate the existence of a transcendent being have been systematically negated in an attempt to obtain Nietzsche's negative ideal of pure nothingness. His premise was that it would then become possible to break through to a transcendent realm of existence and obtain the happiness that cannot be found in traditional philosophy, with its futile preoccupation with "being." But the potentiation of nothingness did not lead to this happy result. It became increasingly evident as Nihilism approached absolute value that there was nothing "beyond good and evil," no transcendent other-realm to break through to after negating all consciousness of being and the good. In fact Nihilism has precisely the same limitations as Idealism and Rationalism. Its ideal of absolute resistance to existent valuations leads to nothingness and no substantive value.

Nihilism negated Transcendentalism progressively, leading to pure nothingness. This is a totalitarian value because it cannot tolerate any intimation of being; hence the lockstep uniformity seen in academic journals at the end of the age and the fevered resistance of the science community to such innocuous concepts as intelligent design. And as was the case with both Idealism and Rationalism, Nihilism rapidly loses its appeal as it reaches totalitarian proportions. Nothingness is a limited value in itself, and Nihilism has proven to be a narrow analytical tool in the arts and sciences. It is capable of generating enthusiasm as long as there are perceived dragons of "being" to be slain but begins to collapse under its own weight when it approaches its own goal of pure nothingness.

The totality that is Nihilism cannot be progressively undone, however—for the very reason that it *is* a totality. Nothing can be subtracted from nothingness. Nihilism is dead, but it is also perfectly impervious to any form of gradualism. The only way to go beyond it is to overthrow it and impose a new construct of being.

The Humanity of the Good

So WHAT's with all of this harrumphing about "the good"? Is it really as inhumane as they say? And is it true that absolute resistance to the good, or Nihilism, can bring about a more humane existence?

Nihilism came into being in the nineteenth century, which certainly had its share of discontents—a time spent in the shadow of chaos as men like Napoleon and Bismark hammered out their destinies through war and brinksmanship; a time of famine and other natural disasters. The unhappy century also saw the rise of industrialism and the growing pains of capitalism, which included inhumane working conditions and ferment among the social classes as the old feudal system broke down and was replaced with something far more fluid and uncertain.

Now as it happened, all of this unhappiness coincided with Hegel's rather optimistic claim that his "scientific synthesis" had rung in the end of intellectual history and was a sign of a golden new age of understanding. Hegel thought his method of constructing being had the power to raise the thinking of philosophers to the level of the Absolute Idea. And it seemed to go as far as any synthetic method could go to resolving the ancient conflict between sense and intellect, since it claimed to have incorporated the nothingness caused by pure intellect into its construct of being as itself.

Hegel's description of his method caused great excitement among the philosophers; it seemed almost everyone was using his concepts and terminology by the middle of the century. But the appearance of the scientific synthesis did not coincide with a sudden outbreak of happiness or bring the troubles of the world to an end. And since the purpose of philosophy is to provide happiness, this failure led to an entirely new kind of resistance, at least in Western culture—resistance to the concept of "being" itself and its implication of transcendent being.

That implication can be traced to Plato, who equated intellect and its capacity to describe being with "the good." Plato saw that the beauty of nature is good, or highly desirable; and it seemed to him that the source of this goodness was divine intellect, which led him to conclude that existence was a combination of matter and the beautiful forms of value furnished by divine intellect, and that unhappiness was the result of the impurity of this mixture. Thus he claimed it was possible to obtain the good of happiness by negating any construct of intellect and matter for the sake of pure mind.

But as his famous student pointed out, this method has the unfortunate effect of resulting in nothingness. Aristotle agreed with Plato that the good is intellect—but if the good is a force of pure resistance to any possible coming-together of intellect and sense, then it negates all existent values. Aristotle attempted to overcome this difficulty by claiming that the sensuous universe is not a mere illusion of goodness but is actually a synthesis of divine intellect and matter. But the problem with his description of the good is that it is precisely in present existence that we find ourselves feeling unhappy.

So the philosophers equated intellect with "the good," a transcendent state of being, and attempted to identify a method of using intellect to obtain the happiness of knowing transcendent being. But their descriptions of "the good" were not transcendent. They were divided between intellect and sense because the goodness of intellect, which is its qualitative force of resistance, is not the same thing as sensuous existence.

This insuperable difference accounts for the cycles seen in philosophy. Each new construct of value gives birth to resistance, and the potentiation of resistance leads to the desire for a new construct of value. Scholasticism, a construct of being that melded Aristotle with Christianity, had been overthrown by Rationalism, which claimed to be capable of disclosing the nature of being through pure intellect and its capacity to doubt any construct of value. But pure doubt led to nothingness in the end—which gave Kant and Hegel the impetus to attempt to cast the synthesis in a new and more dynamic light.

Their construct was to be a "scientific synthesis" without the teleological overtones of Scholasticism. Aristotle's description of the sensuous universe as a synthesis of divine intellect and matter seemed hopelessly antiquated in an age of science and naturalism. So Kant tried to describe a synthesis that takes place in the human mind for its own sake. The transcendent cannot be known if it is pure intellect, according to Kant, but it is possible to obtain "transcendental" value judgments by using a scientific method to look for signs of the transcendent being in the mind and its understanding of being.

Kant set aside the First Cause that was the basis of Aristotle's description of the good and shifted the venue of synthetic method from the mind of God to the human mind; and then Hegel took up this new concept of the synthesis and described a construct of being and nothingness itself—of our concepts of being and our own resistance to the limitations of those concepts. He tried to compensate for the loss of the First Mover by invoking evolution, which had become popular in scientific circles. Supposedly our concepts of being were evolving toward a higher synthesis, and Hegel presented his own synthesis as the summit of this evolutionary process—the end of intellectual history and the search for knowledge of transcendent being.

But Hegel's description of "there-being" was so highly evolved as to be almost incomprehensible. In his eagerness to exhibit resistance to the limitations of all existing constructs of value, he veered into an ethereal rhetorical realm that did not seem to have much of anything to do with being itself—with being as human beings actually know it. In short, his construct was so forbidding that it made transcendent being seem like a bit of a bully. It was nothing like Aristotle's Golden Mean or Thomas's charitable Pure Act, benevolent concepts that mortals could grasp readily and put to good use and from which they could also derive some comfort. In comparison, the Absolute Idea seemed mammoth, baffling, mechanistic, cold.

Hegel made transcendent being seem inhumane. His construct was so difficult to understand that it was almost punitive and added to the burdens of the age. And his opponents used this forbidding difficulty against him. They conceded that his philosophy represented the summit of the evolution of methods of describing "being"—but they found a way to turn evolution against him in Darwin. According to the doctrine of Natural Selection, it was possible to rise to transcendent value without invoking transcendent being. By the light of the new naturalism, philosophy and its concepts of "the good" began to look like they were the *cause* of unhappiness, since they came between humanity and nature.

If, as Darwin's theory suggests, the Absolute Idea does not actually exist, or at least has nothing to do with the values found in nature, then Hegel's forbidding construct of being and nothingness may be literally nothing—a feverish apparition. And in that case it is not necessary to torture oneself with the attempt to understand it. Philosophers like Nietzsche began to suggest that the time had come to negate our pessimism-inducing obsession with such concepts as "being" and "the good" and embrace the transcendent possibilities that seemed to have been bred into us through the survival of the fittest.

Nietzsche's strategy was both simple and brilliant. Since Hegel's concept of being was painfully difficult to understand, he accused it of being inhumane. What sort of God would cruelly torture his creatures with synthetic metaphysics? Meanwhile Darwin's disquisition on religion captured the temper of the age, at least among leading intellectuals. The Supreme Being of philosophers and theologians was punitive and small. Who could accept a God who condemned those who did not believe in him to eternal damnation, including perhaps one's friends and relations?

The notion of Natural Selection suggested that the Absolute Idea had robbed men of the strength and vitality that were their evolutionary birthright by forcing them to aspire to tyrannical metaphysical abstractions. Philosophy and its airy concepts of "the good" imposed an unnatural resistance to the sense realm on creatures who seemed to have obtained their preeminence through nature itself. The way to obtain happiness, then, was to negate this cruel taskmaster and embrace the transcendent principle within—the will to power.

Nihilism—the natural force of resistance to any concept of being found in our awareness of its potential nothingness—was supposed to bring about a more humane existence by annihilating the difference between human existence and the good of happiness. Nietzsche claimed it was possible to cast off our sense of inadequacy and become like Dionysus, a happy bibbler who leads a perfectly carefree natural existence, simply by negating "the good" of the philosophers and theologians.

The idea was that existence had become polluted through the concept of "the good," which divides man against himself and the very qualities that make him strong. And in that case, it seemed possible to restore him to a happy state of being by negating "the good" and encouraging him to embrace his own existence. But Nihilism turned out to be as hard a taskmaster as the scientific synthesis. It liberated the philosopher from Hegel's tyrannical construct of being, but it enslaved him to a Spartan diet of absolute resistance to any thought of being or the good.

Nihilism requires the negation of thinking itself in order to obtain undivided value. Plato launched the age of philosophy by equating intellect and its resistance to unhappiness with "the good" and implying that sensuous existence is evil—the duality of good and evil that troubled Nietzsche. His remedy for this dualism was to undo Plato by embracing the will to power, a unifying power said to be found in sensuous existence for its own sake. But the only way to unify the resistance of sensuous existence to the dualism of philosophy is to annihilate intellect itself, since intellect is different from sense.

Just as it was impossible for sensuous beings to obtain knowledge of an undivided value by negating sense for the sake of pure intellect, so it is impossible for intellectual beings to overcome the dividedness of philosophy by attempting to negate intellect and embrace pure unreflecting existence. Intellect is naturally cognizant of the beauty of a red cardinal in a forsythia bush against a background of snowy white. It immediately recognizes that this beauty is "good," or highly desirable, and it is impossible to prevent it from making such judgments because intellect is a qualitative power by its very nature.

The only way to negate any thought of "the good" is to attempt to annihilate the goodness of the cardinal—which is just what has been done in the Modern age. Thus Nihilism leads to a colorless existence, a gray existence where an attempt is made to obtain transcendence by substituting the will to power for Plato's love of beauty. Ironically, Nihilism had the same net effect as Idealism—it negated the goodness of existent values. It compelled the superman to annihilate the great pleasures of the beauty of nature in order to obtain a state of absolute resistance to "the good."

Nihilism was supposed to produce a more humane existence by negating the difference between "being"—which implies transcendent being—and human beings. The idea was that "being" was inhuman because it was unlike human existence. And since *being* intimates life, the negation of being also requires negating the value of life. This is just what Nietzsche admonished the superman to do. He must give up any thought of the transcendent value that the philosophers attributed to being and embrace his mortality in order to totalize the resistance provided by nothingness.

But then Nihilism introduces a morbid and inhuman quality into the modern identity. The gloominess of the superman bears little resemblance to the carefree god of wine that Nietzsche loved. Dionysus is happy for two reasons. First, he is immortal; there is no consciousness of powerlessness to impede him. But also he has been set apart from the court of the gods and their perpetual power struggle. He represents an inchoate recognition of the limitations of the will to power. The gods that were created by men struggle for domination just as men struggle. Men are afraid of the nothingness of the grave, and this fear causes them to attempt to justify their existence through domination.

But it is impossible to find happiness through the will to dominate. The pantheon of Homer was a desperate place. It seems that when poets tried to imagine a *happy* god, like Dionysus, they found it necessary to separate him from the court of the gods through the jealous rage of Hera. He was a wanderer who spread joy and civilization by teaching the cultivation of wine. His happiness—the difference between him and the desperation on display on Mt Olympus—is obtained first of all through life, as the twice-born god, and also through the peace that came to him fortuitously by being compelled to give up the opportunity to dominate his fellow immortals.

But Nietzsche attempted to obtain happiness in just the opposite way from his favorite god—by negating the value of life and embracing the will to power. Nihilism was supposed to produce a more humane existence by negating the difference between "the good" and human existence, but the only way to justify the identity of the superman after the negation of the good is through the will to power. And while the will to power may be more *human* than the concepts of the good seen in philosophy, it is not more *humane*. It requires the negation of such values as kindness and pity—values that are humane in the highest sense because they build up human beings.

Nietzsche made it quite clear that the superman must give up kindness and pity in order to become a superman, since these values come into direct conflict with the will to dominate. In fact Nihilism requires giving up all of the great qualities that are entailed in a consciousness of the value of life—such as gentleness, magnanimity, humility, tenderness and mercy. But while it may be possible to muscle Hegel's "superior man" and his muddled middle terms out of the public square by eschewing such qualities, it is impossible to obtain the transcendent identity of the "superman," since they are the greatest values known to man.

The limitations of the superman have now become quite obvious. Absolute resistance to being and "the good" did not lead to a more humane existence. Nihilism generated a great deal of enthusiasm through the notion that it was possible to break through to some unimaginably desirable state of existence by negating the tyranny of the good. In fact just the opposite occurred. The negation of the good led to a gray thought-existence and culture, while the negation of such life-giving values as kindness and pity led to the iron-fisted inhumanity of the modern age.

The superman was no less inhumane than the concepts of "the good" seen in philosophy. Like them, he attempted to obtain a transcendent identity through intellect and its capacity for judgment—but judgment is an annihilating power. Plato's Highest Good was inhumane because it was a force of pure resistance to flesh-and-blood humanity. Aristotle's Supreme Being was inhumane because it compelled humans to overcome the difference between itself and their existence through pure action—which is impossible if, as he claims, Supreme Being is "life itself." And the superman was inhumane because he sought to justify his existence through the will to power, by dominating others and depriving them of life.

Philosophy has destroyed itself through its excessive love of intellect. It is self-defeating to deny the goodness of the cardinal or such humane values as kindness and pity. After the self-immolation of philosophy through Nihilism, we find ourselves standing at square one again—except this time our innocence is the product of experience. We are fully aware of the limitations of intellect; indeed, we are the first-born of those limitations. Thus it has become possible to put philosophy behind us and see if there is a way to restore the great values that we ourselves destroyed.

If we are willing to give up the value judgments about "the good" seen in Plato and Aristotle, then we are also free to set aside the superman and his ideal of absolute resistance to the good. We are free to see what we see with our own eyes, unmediated by philosophy and the attempt to equate intellect with a transcendent power. Plato said that our eyes deceive us, but Plato himself was deceived by his excessive love of intellect. It is not the cardinal that is a delusion; it is the vanity of thinking we can use intellect and its capacity for resistance to make ourselves into transcendent beings.

It is a strange property of eyes that they present such vivid images to the mind as a red cardinal in a snowy bush. Unfocus brings focus into focus. We are perfectly free now to luxuriate in such great pleasures because philosophy has annihilated itself—as long as we are willing to set aside the vanity of its love of judgment. It was as if we had awoken from a strange dream. For a long time we were confused about the goodness of nature and made ourselves miserable by arguing about it. But the cardinal was there all along—and will still be there long after our wrangling over "the good" has been forgotten.

"I restored that which I did not take away." But then which is more humane? The Nihilism that compels us to attempt to suppress any thought of the goodness of the cardinal and makes the world colorless and gray, or the power that restores those pleasures at the very moment that we become willing to give up our excessive love of intellect?

The Vessel

STILL TODAY the artist is said to "follow his muse." Of course no one really thinks of the muse as a supernatural being anymore; the word has long since been relegated to the musty realm of metaphor. But there can be no doubt that *something* directs the pen of writers, or it would be impossible to talk about such things as the Renaissance or Romanticism. That something is the culture itself—the vessel into which the artist pours his art.

It seems he has little choice in the matter, poor fellow. Either he has to seek being in the prevailing culture or accept the nothingness that comes with attempting to resist it. This is because the prevailing culture reflects the *fear* of nothingness. All mortals desire an identity that is larger than their mortality, and the prevailing culture supplies such an identity for the simple reason that it is prevalent. The power that makes it prevalent also makes it seem equal to the desire for a transcendent identity and offers a path of least resistance to those who are seeking to make a name for themselves.

Unfortunately that appearance of transcendent power is an illusion. All cultural identities are rooted in intellect and its capacity for resistance, and therefore all cultural identities are divided in desirability. In fact Western history can be described as a series of cycles in which each new age attempts to obtain a transcendent identity through resistance to the limitations of the one that preceded it. The Renaissance and Reformation came into being through resistance to Scholasticism, and the age of Empiricism through resistance to Renaissance Neoplatonism, and Rationalism to Empiricism, and Romanticism to Rationalism, and now Nihilism to Romanticism.

These identities are not without appeal or they never would have become powerful in the first place. But since they are rooted in resistance, they lead to divided values, and their own limitations become evident over time. Rationalism was an enticing identity because Descartes' love of pure reason seemed fresh and new after the fatiguing construct of being produced by Scholasticism. But the capacity of intellect to doubt any construct of value cannot produce a concrete description of being. When Rationalism devolves to the point where Hume claims that literally nothing of value to the philosopher can be learned from nature, its love of pure intellect begins to wear thin, making it vulnerable to a new form of resistance.

That resistance came in the form of Kant and the Transcendental Aesthetic, a self-described "constructive" method that attempted to overcome the limitations of Rationalism by teasing out middle terms between its critical force of resistance and Empiricism, which is rooted in the goodness of nature. This construct of value became the vessel of Romanticism. Just as Pope and Haydn and Reynolds and Rousseau had found a voice in the prevailing culture by trimming their sails to Rationalism and its love of pure reason, so Goethe and Wordsworth and Beethoven and Hegel sought identity in Romanticism and the concept of a synthesis of resistance and existent values.

Hegel claimed that this new construct had the power to put an end to the cycles of intellectual history by mediating between being and nothingness. The problem in philosophy is that intellect is a qualitative force of resistance—it is not the same thing as sense. There is a *difference* between intellect and sense, and this difference leaves the door open for resistance to the validity of the value judgments intellect produces about the sensuous universe. When this resistance is carried to the extreme seen in Hume, it results in nothingness, or the annihilation of all constructs of value.

Hegel claimed that it was possible to overcome this difficulty by giving nothingness full status in philosophy and describing its limits. If it were possible to assign a limit to nothingness, then it would be possible to overcome its force of resistance and describe a construct of being and nothingness itself. But it is impossible for the synthetic philosopher to overcome the power of nothingness over the imagination once he concedes that it is real. This was shown by Hegel's own construct. His attempt at overcoming nothingness and its force of resistance led to metaphysics so abstruse and difficult that they began to seem like nothing.

Any attempt to describe a construct of intellect and sense leads to fatiguing results because of the difference between these values, but Hegel's synthesis was far more forbidding than anything seen in Aristotle or Thomas because he attempted to take the construct of being out of the mind of God and put it in the human mind. All of the burden of holding being and nothingness together fell on human beings themselves and their ability to wield Hegel's method—which was so burdensome as to seem intolerable. Meanwhile the glorification of nature that was the basis of Romanticism was becoming a little stale. There can be no question that flowers are highly desirable, but the human spirit can only endure just so much flowery poetry before it begins to long for a cold, bracing bath.

Enter the superman on the stage of history and a new and more radical form of resistance. Nietzsche claimed that Hegel's construct of "being" was leading to pessimism by making it seem impossibly difficult. Besides, Darwin had made any such construct seem unnecessary by describing a force in nature that appeared to lead to transcendent values without the help of a transcendent being. According to Darwin, nature is producing a higher state of being of its own accord through the survival of the fittest; and Nietzsche took up the nothingness of this natural power to suggest that it was possible to find happiness by annihilating philosophy and its preoccupation with being.

Nihilism came into being through resistance to the limitations of Romanticism and its construct of value. Just as Rationalism had seemed to provide a fresh, new beginning by overturning the ponderous construct of being that was Scholasticism, so the appeal of Nihilism was based on its power to overturn the fatiguing construct of there-being described by Hegel. Indeed, Nihilism seemed even fresher than Rationalism to its denizens because it negated "being" itself—something new, at least in the West. This bold step was supposed to liberate the philosopher from the limitations of philosophy and launch him into uncharted waters.

But those waters were not quite as uncharted as they seemed. Philosophy bases its promises of happiness on intellect and its capacity for resistance, but then any iteration of philosophy leads to a divide between pure resistance and the attempt to find happiness in a construct of resistance and existent values. Rationalism could not produce a transcendent identity by using pure resistance to undo Scholasticism because pure resistance leads to nothingness—nor can Nihilism produce a "transvaluation of value" by embracing nothingness itself because nothingness negates the value of being.

Nihilism launched philosophy on very much the same path as Rationalism, the path of pure resistance, but it led to more limited results than Rationalism by attempting to negate "being" and "the good" as if they did not exist. The identity of the superman is based on his capacity to annihilate any thought of "the good," or transcendent being, and seek a transcendent identity in the will to dominate; but then his own harsh ideal of pure nothingness requires him to attempt to negate the goodness of existent values—which is impossible. The goodness of nature cannot be negated because that goodness is real. Nature, a being or existent value, is left over from Nihilism and its annihilating force of resistance and exposes the nothingness of the superman.

The limitations of Nihilism are becoming quite obvious at the end of the age because Nietzsche based the identity of the superman on the will to dominate. Nihilism negated God, the dominus, since the descriptions of transcendent being seen in philosophy were divided between resistance and existence. But if God or "being" is negated in philosophy, then it is no longer possible to obtain precedence through one's methods of describing being. Some new measure of value was necessary in order to validate the superman and his claim to transcendence, and Nietzsche thought he had found such a value in the "survival of the fittest," which he translated into the will to power.

The notion was that the will to dominate was a real value found in nature. It was different from "being" because it did not exist outside human beings—it was, according to Darwin, part of their very evolutionary make-up. Also Darwinism suggested that the law of the survival of the fittest was somehow leading to a glorious conclusion and that evolution was in the process of producing a transcendent state of natural existence. Thus it seemed to Nietzsche that it was possible to go beyond the dividedness seen in philosophy and its concepts of being by embracing the will to power that seemed by Darwinian logic to distinguish men and annihilating any thought of "being."

The old philosophers tried to dominate each other through their descriptions of "being" and "the good." Nietzsche claimed it was possible to go beyond their dividedness by negating the good and embracing domination for its own sake. But then there are only two ways for the superman to justify the high opinion he has of himself—either through domination on the battlefield or in culture. Nietzsche's romantic notions of warfare became outdated with the First World War, which rendered individual effort almost meaningless. But neither was the superman able to obtain domination in the less overtly violent realm of the arts. He was not able to dominate the Romantics through his ideal of absolute resistance to the good. Indeed, now that the novelty of his identity has worn off it would seem that the Romantics have begun to dominate *him*.

A quick glance at the concert hall, for example, clearly indicates that the superman has not obtained the domination he seeks. Romanticism continues to hold center stage, even though it has long since lost its freshness. Perhaps it is not reasonable to look for a Beethoven or a Brahms in every age, but even the lesser lights of Romanticism have begun to dominate the poor superman at the end of the age—Schubert, Schumann,

Chopin, Liszt, Mendelssohn, Wagner, Verdi, Dvorak, Bruckner. It seems unlikely that *all* of these composers were more gifted than their Modern counterparts. No, a more likely explanation is that Romanticism provided a more felicitous cultural vessel than Nihilism.

The Romantics had a more desirable form into which to pour their art than the poor superman, who finds himself in the unenviable position of having to seek identity in the annihilation of all existent values. Nature was the muse of the Romantics, and no reasonable person doubts that nature is highly desirable. Any spring day is worthy of a Pastoral Symphony; any towering mountain can bring forth a Prelude; any nightingale is deserving of an Ode and the highest oblation poets can offer. Nature is not the transcendent value that synthetic philosophers made it out to be—it is mortal, after all—but the loveliness of nature provides a solid footing for the muse pursued by such artists as Wordsworth and Beethoven.

Nature is a worthy muse because it is highly desirable—it is "good." But the superman attempts to follow the muse of absolute resistance to the good, which makes it impossible for him to produce art that is highly desirable. The ultimate standard of value in art is desirability, and by this standard it seems that the superman is encountering some difficulty in his quest to obtain domination. He must annihilate the love of nature seen in Romanticism in order to dominate it—but this requires the poor fellow to resist the natural musical values of melody, harmony and rhythm, which leads to music that is most unnatural.

In short, the problem with the superman and his ideal of absolute resistance to "the good" is that goodness is the essence of desirability. Nothing that is not good can be desirable, and nothing that is not desirable can be good. The superman can create art that is *different* from Romanticism by negating the good, but this same ideal of pure resistance also prevents him from creating art that is highly desirable. His desire to obtain domination by negating the good leads to art that is lacking in the very thing that makes art attractive in the first place, which is desirability.

Haydn and Mozart also lived in an age that was in love with pure intellect and its capacity for resistance—but Rationalism did not lead to the annihilation of music because it was not based on absolute resistance to the good. Descartes opposed Scholasticism, but he did not oppose the Schoolmen's God. He wanted to use the mind's capacity for resistance to refine the description of being that resulted from Scholasticism, not to annihilate being itself. Thus composers who followed the muse of Rationalism sought identity in the refining power of the line of beauty and its resistance to polyphony.

But the supermen are not refiners—they are a refining fire. They are "new gods," and they come with lightening bolts in their hands. Their goal was not to improve upon the stem of being through careful pruning; they wanted to pull it up by the roots and cast it into the fire. But the plant cannot bear fruit once it has been torn up. The superman was unable to obtain the domination he desired through absolute resistance to being because the annihilation of being leads to nothingness. The goodness of such things as melody, harmony and rhythm reveals his limitations and deprives him of the happiness he seeks.

The cultural vessel that is Modernism failed to produce the domination sought by the superman. And because he cannot dominate, his identity fails to live up to its promise and loses its forcefulness. The same love of domination that informed his art and culture has now begun to work against him by exposing his fatal limitations.

Mozart's Muse

PITY THE poor Modern composer. It wasn't too long ago that Tchaikovsky and Puccini were churning out melodies that could be heard on the lips of draymen in the park and the baker at his oven—and yet their music also somehow managed to find its way into the concert hall, where it did not seem so out of place. Not so in the "modern" era, however. Music has diverged along two highly incompatible paths. The masses became awash in popular music, defined by its very accessibility, while serious composers were forced into the mold of the avant-garde— i.e., that which is highly inaccessible to the masses.

The absolute character of this divergence is something new. There has always been an element of elitism in serious music, of course, but such composers as Bach, Handel, Mozart, Beethoven and Verdi were not compelled by their cultural identities to actively resist popular acceptance; to shun it like the plague, as is the case with "modern" composers. Serious music is differentiated from mass culture by its very nature, but Modern music became doubly differentiated by the nature of Modernism itself— and by a momentous economic change that took the elites by surprise.

Modernism is based on Nihilism, or the concept that absolute resistance to "the good" is capable of producing transcendent value. This concept reflects the failure of the philosophers to provide an undivided description of the good. Plato and Aristotle equated the good with intellect and its resistance to divided values, but this resistance cannot be used to obtain knowledge of any undivided value because intellect is different from sense. When it became apparent that the philosophers were unable to overcome this difference through any method of describing value, Nietzsche tried to go beyond the limitations of philosophy by negating the good and embracing the will to power.

Nietzsche succeeded in negating philosophy and the dividedness of its value judgments about the good, but his ideal of absolute resistance to the good led to highly divided values in its own right because the word *good* indicates more than just "the good." Plato and Aristotle equated "the good" with intellect, but the word *good* simply indicates desirability. Intellect and sense are both good—highly desirable—for their own sake, which is why the attempt to equate intellect with the good leads to divided value judgments in philosophy. But in their eagerness to go beyond the dividedness of philosophy by negating the good, the Nihilists negated desirability itself.

This has tangible consequences, as became evident when Nihilism found its way into the arts. Absolute resistance to the good has a devastating impact on music because it requires the negation of the goodness of all existent values. If the good quite literally does not exist, then there can be no goodness in such things as melody, harmony, or rhythm. The superman must exhibit absolute resistance to very notion of their goodness in order to obtain a place in the hallowed halls of Modernism. But then Nihilism is self-limiting, since it is impossible to compose music that is highly desirable by negating melody, harmony and rhythm—the very substance of music—as if they had no value.

Nihilism obtained popularity through resistance to the "herd mentality" that resulted, in Nietzsche's view, from Hegel's scientific synthesis. All synthetic methods reflect the idea that happiness can be found in identifying middle terms between intellect and sense. For his own part, Hegel tried to describe a synthesis of Empiricism and Rationalism, of scientific concepts of "being" based on the senses and the capacity of intellect for resistance to the limitations of those concepts, or to conceive of their nothingness.

Hegel's synthesis of being and nothingness helped to enshrine the Transcendental Aesthetic, but Nietzsche found a way to overthrow it—with an assist from Darwin—by negating transcendent being and embracing nothingness for its own sake. The notion of the survival of the fittest seemed to account for the goodness of the species without having to invoke a transcendent being, and Nietzsche used this nothingness to negate Transcendentalism in favor of the will to power. Philosophy's descriptions of the good were divided between sense and intellect, but the premise of Nihilism is that the superman can go beyond this dividedness by taking up absolute resistance to the good and seeking transcendent value in human existence for its own sake.

Nihilism provided a timely outlet for opposition that had been growing to Hegel and the mind-numbing determinism of his synthesis. But Nietzsche was able to make the concept of absolute resistance to "the good" seem especially appealing through a historical coincidence that had nothing to do with Hegel. The ascendance of Hegel's synthesis just happened to occur at the same time as the rise of industrial capitalism and the new middle class, which was perceived by the cultural elite as a threat to its exalted status; Nietzsche exploited this insecurity brilliantly by linking Nihilism's resistance to Hegel's middle terms to resistance to the "herd mentality" of the middle class.

The middle class was relatively small at the time, which is why many leading thinkers were confident that it could be overthrown. But then something happened that they did not anticipate. Cheap energy and industrialization brought about a steady expansion of the middle class to the point where it appropriated much of the working class and began to dominate society. And then the same synergy that Nietzsche had sought by linking Nihilism to resistance to the middle class began to lead to a doubly-differentiated elitism. "Modern" artists found themselves bucking a donkey that grew larger and larger until they became like fleas on its back and were reduced to biting and annoying.

This effect is evident in Modern music. The rise of the middle class led to an explosion of popular music, attracting such composers as Gershwin and Porter and Ellington. At the same time a whole new arena for composers came into being through cinema. Wagner's dream was fulfilled as film came to depend heavily on music for a sense of drama. Movies are a popular art form by necessity, because of the costs involved, but such composers as Korngold, Bernstein and Williams are something more than popular musicians. And the imperative of having to resist everything that makes them appealing would put a considerable strain on Beethoven himself.

Meanwhile the cultural elite resisted this groundswell of popular culture by turning the concert hall into a fortress. Modern music became characterized by an attempt to validate the transcendent status of the superman through a conspicuous show of resistance to the pleasures of the common herd, leading to a sharp divide between serious music and anything that might be deemed popular. Composers found it impossible to embrace melody, harmony and rhythm and also find a voice in the concert hall, which was reserved for the avant-garde. Indeed, Schoenberg gained notoriety by claiming to have banished such composers through his twelve-tone row.

The superman obtained domination in the concert hall through the will to power; Nihilism continues to dictate much of what Modern composers are permitted to write as well as what music lovers are permitted to hear. But the attempt to obtain a transcendent identity by resisting the pleasures of an expanding middle class has turned into a death-wish. An insistence on open contempt for middle class values makes it impossible for a new Mozart or Beethoven to emerge—composers who appeal to mere mortals as well as to supermen. For that matter, most of what is heard today *is* Mozart and Beethoven. The concert hall becomes a preservation trust, perpetuating itself by trading on past glories.

Classical music found itself in this unwholesome predicament through the vanity of philosophy and the dividedness of its cultural identities. The love of pure intellect that epitomized the Enlightenment led to a celebration of form and refinement; to a degree of resistance to the sensuous qualities of music. Transcendentalism led to nature-worship and a corresponding loss of form and emotional restraint. And then Nihilism attempted to go "beyond" the dividedness of these identities by declaring that God was dead and destroying Valhalla. The superman made himself into an all-consuming fire that reduced Western culture and its devotion to "the good" to ashes, but this same withering force of resistance also prevented him from producing a musical idiom that was good or highly desirable for its own sake.

And yet it is still possible for something new to rise up from the ashes of Western culture—for the very reason that they *are* ashes. Nihilism is a sign of a collective awareness of the limitations of philosophy and the inability of intellect to provide knowledge of what is good. It annihilates the old equation of intellect with the good, which leads to the divided values seen in philosophy. But by barring the door to the thought-world of Plato and Aristotle, it opens up a new sphere of possibility for the composer—because the power that makes music seem "good" is not intellect. It is desirability itself.

This is the power referred to by Augustine as "love itself." Philosophy is the love of knowledge, but "love itself" is different from the divided loves seen in philosophy because it is not rooted in the differential power of intellect. Plato and Aristotle sought the identity of lovers of the good through intellect and its force of judgment, but this same power also divides intellect from sense. Plato was in love with the idea that the good is pure intellect, while Aristotle was in love with the notion of describing the good as a synthesis of intellect and sense. These concepts of the good were divided between intellect and sense, divided by the very nature of intellect itself and its capacity for qualitative resistance; but "love itself" does not divide them, since both are highly desirable.

No new philosophy of "the good" can emerge after Nihilism because Nihilism constitutes an acknowledgment that the excessive love of intellect seen in philosophy leads to divided concepts of value. Nihilism is the natural denouement of philosophy, which is why composers who continue to cling to intellect and its differential force of resistance are compelled to perpetuate the clichés of the superman and his ideal of absolute resistance to the good. But "love itself" provides knowledge of value through desirability for its own sake, not through intellect. Thus it provides the composer with an opportunity to go beyond the limitations of Nihilism and explore new realms of possibility.

Let him sit at the piano, then, and let him rest his fingers on the cool, quiescent keys. His time has come—and it may be uniquely *his* time, for reasons that will become clear in a moment. But before he begins to play, let him pause for a moment to allow the great conflagration of Western culture and its excessive love of intellect to rise up into his soul; not just of Rationalism and Romanticism but also of the superman and the self-negating vanity of the will to power. And then let him remember Mozart's claim that the soul of genius is "love, love, love."

According to Mozart, there is a muse in music which is not the same thing as intellect, the first love of the philosophers. His use of the threefold emphasis suggests that this was a muse of which he himself had first-hand knowledge, a real force in existence that could be accessed during the act of composition and not merely a poetic fiction. And in that case Mozart's muse has momentous implications for composers—because "love, love, love" is not the same thing as intellect. If such a muse exists, then they are not compelled to follow the muse of the superman and his love of nothingness. There is another muse they can follow that does not reflect the excessive love of intellect seen in philosophy and does not lead to annihilation in the end.

The question, then, is whether Mozart was right. Is there really such a muse? And does it have the power to go beyond the dividedness of sense and intellect seen in philosophy? Composers are in a unique position to test this proposition because music is not just intellect but also a sensuous thing. The philosophers thought that the goodness of existent values—the beauty and excellence of nature—was a sign of the qualitative power of a divine Intellect that imposed its forms of value on matter. It is no longer possible to think of nature as a combination of intellect and matter; but Mozart's description of creative genius indicates the existence of a formative power that is not the same thing as intellect and has nothing to do with the value judgments seen in philosophy. "Love, love, love" obtains postmodern resonance through the formulation *deus caritas est*.

If it is possible to create highly desirable music by following the muse of "love, love, love," as Mozart suggested, then this may indicate that the true form of the goodness of existent values is love itself and not intellect, as the philosophers claimed. And in that case there would appear to be a way of obtaining knowledge of what is good that is not the same thing as intellect or its methods of judging value. Love provides knowledge of value through its discriminating power. It does not depend upon intellect to empower knowledge, and therefore it is not divided by the difference between intellect and sense.

One immediate benefit of following "love, love, love" is that it provides freedom from the bondage of the will to power. The superman predicated his identity on his ability to dominate; in music, he attempted to demonstrate domination through a show of stout resistance to the masses and their pleasures. "Love, love, love" breaks down this wall between the composer and his audience. The will of love is to serve and give pleasure, not to dominate; to heal and refresh, not to destroy. Mozart's muse liberates the composer from the tyranny of Modernism and the limitations of the will to power.

Let our composer sit down at the piano, then, and let him sound any note in the middle range, the range of his own voice, and begin to experiment with the power of Mozart's muse to inform a melody that goes beyond the annihilation of Western intellectual tradition. The first thing to be discovered through such an experiment is that "love, love, love" is more than just a lovely idea; it is a fact of existence. If he wants to restore the attractive power of melody to music, he cannot leave the safety of that first note and go on to play another without allowing Mozart's muse to inform his choice. The will to power is not adequate for the restoration of melody. He must follow another will which is revealed through desirability, a real power that establishes definite boundaries in music.

Following Mozart's muse leads to the discovery that there are indeed laws governing the values found in sensuous existence. The superman's claim that there is no such thing as "the good" may be valid within the narrow confines of philosophy—it is impossible to justify the transcendent being described by Plato and Aristotle, which is intellect in its essence—but it is also true that the composer must follow a muse not found in his own mind or will in order to create a desirable melody. The reality of this muse was indisputable to Mozart. And it is shown today by the fact that the composer cannot resist it and also produce desirable results.

Mozart's muse provides the means of reconciling intellect and sense that cannot be found in intellect or its methods. Music is a sensuous thing, but the postmodern composer cannot follow the muse of "love, love, love" without fully incorporating Nihilism and the burning of Valhalla into his melody—his own innate resistance to the limitations of the cultural identities of the past. It is impossible to restore the attractive power of melody by attempting to revert to Rationalism or Romanticism. The limitations of those identities have become too obvious to satisfy the human spirit. The restoration of music requires the composer to fully include Nihilism and its resistance to the dividedness of those identities into his melody even as it is in the process of coming into being.

The new music waiting to be created through Mozart's muse must go beyond the limitations of Rationalism and Romanticism as well as the superman and his love of nothingness. And in fact this resistance to worn-out identities can be seen in Mozart himself. His early compositions re-flected the love of form and purity of line dictated by Rationalism, which was based on a belief in the purifying power of reason. This belief was manifested in the resistance of Neoclassical music to Baroque ornamen-tation and polyphony. By the end of his brief life, however, Mozart had begun to move beyond the stifling limitations of his own age. Through his study of Bach and Handel, he discovered the power of polyphony to add weight and substance to the line of beauty—a discovery that was directly responsible for the quantum leap seen in his last compositions.

On a cautionary note, it should be pointed out that Mozart's in-creasing willingness to follow the muse of "love, love, love" seems to have corresponded with a decrease in popularity and earning power. The same compositions that have the power to astonish audiences today also alien-ated the audiences of his own time because they were too forward-look-ing. There seems to have been an increasing burden of unhappiness in Mozart's last years which drove him to shatter his own comfort and seek a better muse than the Neoclassicism and virtuosity that made him famous. Perhaps he was in the process of turning away from the false god of fame and fortune that drove him as a young man and seeking happiness in the exalted muse of "love, love, love."

The same muse that led Mozart beyond the limitations of the age of the virtuoso also deprived him of popularity by compelling him to resist the conventions of his day. But this is true of great composers in general. Their greatness was not as apparent to their contemporaries as it is today because they were following a muse that led them beyond the limitations of their own age. Let the postmodern composer count the costs, then, if he desires to follow Mozart's muse. His resistance to the limitations of Nihilism is not likely to endear him to the supermen of Modernism, who continue to cling with vicious glee to their fleeting hegemony. The com-poser who wants to follow Mozart's muse must understand that the world is what it is. It is vanity that rules the world, not love.

Liberation Aesthetics

So what happened was that Nihilism obtained hegemony in modern culture by claiming to have the power to produce transcendent value. But it tried to obtain this value through the negative ideal of absolute resistance to "the good," which leads to nothingness itself. Thus Nihilism wound up having similar aesthetic limitations to Idealism—and to any identity rooted in the love of resistance.

The problem that plagued philosophy from the time of Plato was the dividedness caused by his equation of intellect and its resistance to the unhappiness of existence with "the good," a transcendent value. When totalized, this force of resistance results in the annihilation of all existent values—in nothingness, a value in which there is no aesthetic content. It also results in dualism: according to Plato, intellect is good and sensuous existence is evil. Aristotle tried to overcome this dualism by characterizing the goodness of nature as a ratio of intellectual and material causes, but the problem with Aristotle's concept of the good is that he had to discount some of the force of resistance found in intellect in order get past its negativity and draw it into existence.

Fast forward to Hegel, and the problem remains the same. Rationalism led to nothingness through the negative power of the cogito and its resistance to sense-grounded valuations. Hegel thought he could overcome this nothingness by describing a construct of nothingness and being—but his synthesis had the same limitation as Aristotle. It is impossible to describe such a construct without assigning a limit to nothingness and thus negating its power to resist the limitations of our concepts of being.

Hegel's failure to limit the power of nothingness for the sake of being gave Nietzsche a clever idea. What if the superman were to embrace nothingness instead of being? What if he were to use the force of resistance found in nothingness to annihilate all concepts of being? Would it then become possible to go beyond the dividedness seen in philosophy? Darwinism gave impetus to Nihilism by purporting to show that nature was in the process of evolving transcendent values without the help of a transcendent being. In that case the superman did not need "being" to obtain happiness. All he needed was to embrace the will to power that seemed implicit in the survival of the fittest.

By negating God or "the good," Nihilism appeared to eliminate the dualism caused by Plato's equation of intellect with the good. It appeared to provide the power to go beyond the dividedness of good and evil seen in philosophy and render a "transvaluation of value." In reality, however, Nihilism produced a new form of dualism—by negating the goodness of existent values. There can be no goodness in nature if the good quite literally does not exist; thus Nihilism and its ideal of absolute resistance to the good led to very much the same conclusion as Idealism. Transcendent value is attributed wholly to "nihilism," or intellect and its capacity for resistance—nature is nothing.

The negative effects of this neo-dualism can be seen in Leopold Bloom and his famous outhouse. This was a new way of introducing one's hero, representing a vertical interruption of the overly refined constructs of value associated with the Transcendental Aesthetic. If the practical result of Transcendentalism is the small-minded preoccupation with manners and morals seen in Victorian England and Dublin—an identity made up of sexual repression and grandiose representations of existence—then Bloom's outhouse can generate a good deal of literary value through its capacity to annihilate that stultifying identity and to show the "superior man" with his pants down, as it were.

Bloom in the outhouse provides a devastating force of resistance to the flowery primness of the Victorian drawing room. Here is something about him that is real and has nothing to do with the fine ideals that had been sprinkled through Europe in the wake of Kant and his categorical imperatives. And the naturalism of the outhouse suggests something more as well—the transcendent potential of nothingness. Bloom seems at peace in the rising odor of his ordure, far away from the puppet shows of human existence. The modernists opposed the love of nature seen in the Romantics with a militant naturalism. The old philosophers had divided the psyche between good and evil by equating intellect with the good, but the purpose of the new philosophy was to smash that dualism by annihilating any thought of the good and embracing sensuous existence for its own sake.

According to Nietzsche, it is possible to obtain happiness by negating "the good," the transcendent being, because there is a transcendent principle in existence for its own sake—the will to power. In his mind, this will was best demonstrated on the battlefield, where domination is shorn of subtlety and ambiguity. Now of course Leopold Bloom is not a warrior in any sense of the word; indeed, he seems closer to Quixote than Achilles. But another story about the superman is found in the virtuoso demonstration of his foolishness and shortcomings. The introduction of Bloom in the outhouse introduces the concept of the superman-artist who takes up the cudgel of Nihilism to destroy the phoniness of all forms of transcendentalism and dominate his fellow writers.

But the outhouse scene also demonstrates that the superman-artist is a self-limiting identity. The will to power is not the only value found in existence. It is possible to embrace the outhouse as the antithesis of Transcendentalism and its overwrought celebration of nature, but the aesthetics of the outhouse are purely negative. An outhouse can seem refreshing to the mind when it reflects the mind's own resistance to the limitations of Victorian prudery, but in its *sensuous* self it is not very refreshing at all. Thus the outhouse reveals the dividedness of Nihilism and the attempt to obtain a transcendent identity through intellect and its capacity for pure resistance. Joyce uses the foulness of the outhouse to undermine Western storytelling and its flowery notions of being—but that same foulness prevents it from obtaining transcendent value.

There are roses in existence as well as outhouses, which is why it is impossible for the superman to obtain the transcendent identity he covets through his negative ideal of absolute resistance to the good. Nihilism cannot negate our consciousness of the good because the goodness of roses is a fact of existence. The superman sees thought-existence as an unhappy mixture of the will to power and the falsifications of existence produced by philosophy and its notions of the good—but the goodness of nature is real and cannot be negated. Thus Nihilism leads to a new form of dualism.

This dualism is tyrannical. Plato tried to use the force of resistance found in unhappiness to liberate the philosopher from sense and obtain an ideal of pure intellect, but his followers wound up being trapped in perpetual resistance, perpetual unhappiness, because it is impossible for embodied beings to become pure minds. Similarly the Nihilists predicated transcendence on absolute resistance to the good; but since it is impossible to negate the goodness of nature, they found themselves trapped in a state of permanent resistance.

This predicament is seen in poor Stephen Dedalus as he wanders on the strand. Stephen is miserable, it seems; so miserable that he remains impervious to the manifold enchantments of the seashore. Where other mortals may obtain pleasure from the beauty of the beach and music of the salty waves, Stephen is determined to see nothing but ugliness and alienation. No ocean pleasures are permitted to enter his consciousness as he focuses on "a bloated carcass of a dog lay lolled on bladderwrack" and other such dreary images. On and on he walks with the beauty of nature all around him, seeing nothing but signs of putrefaction.

Now it is true that Stephen's gloom and sense of alienation are facts of existence. But it is also true that he makes his gloominess worse by actively resisting the desirability of nature and focusing exclusively on intellect and its capacity for negation. Stephen is seeking a transcendent identity in Nihilism and its heroic resistance to Transcendentalism, which resistance requires him to annihilate any thought of the goodness of nature. He must attempt to focus on signs of decay in order to avoid becoming conscious of that goodness and slipping back into the dividedness of good and evil.

It is not remarkable that he finds things on the beach to disgust him; what is remarkable is that he ever manages to get off the beach. We see him walking and walking in search of signs to validate the identity of absolute resistance to the good until the episode finally comes to the abrupt conclusion dictated by the finitude of the world's forests and paper supplies. Were this the real world, however, and not a novel, then there would be no end to such a walk—because the goodness of the beach cannot be negated. With each successive step he would find himself enmeshed in the same old drama over and over again. The beach lures him with its pleasures, making it necessary to find another bloated carcass to validate his love of resistance.

Poor Stephen is stuck on the beach because he is clinging to intellect and its capacity to provide a satisfactory identity. It is impossible to overcome the difference between sense and intellect by linking intellect to the good and negating sense—and equally impossible to go "beyond good and evil" by attempting to negate the good as if it did not exist, since the goodness of nature is a fact of existence. Idealism is dead, but Stephen cannot get off the beach by clinging to Nihilism and the dualism produced by its love of resistance. He becomes mired in Nihilism for its own sake—which is not at all the happy outcome that Nietzsche had in mind for modern man.

All cultural identities are obtained through the force of resistance provided by judgment. Lovers of pure resistance and absolute values gain hegemony by annihilating existing constructs of value, and then lovers of synthetic logic strive to put the purists in their place by claiming to have discovered some new way of constructing being. But what if Stephen were to give up all methods of distinguishing men and their thinking? What if he were willing to give up the desire to use intellect and its force of resistance to make himself seem more important than the "superior man" of Hegel? At that point he would obtain freedom from the limitations of judgment. It would no longer be necessary for him to cling to nothingness and its power to resist the goodness of being.

The jaws of the trap that he set for himself would spring open, leaving him free to enjoy the ocean for what it is instead of worrying about what people *think* it is—and what they think about him. After all, the great beauty of the ocean is real and cannot be denied. It has not lost any of its desirability, in spite of Nihilism and the insufferable vanity of the superman. Poor Stephen has been stuck on the beach all these years getting himself tangled in the effluvia of low tide and the rotting carcass of somebody's abandoned dog. That tide has been out for a long time now—but it won't stay out forever. And when it returns, the superman will wash away like a bad dream.

Coda

WHAT EVER happened to the language of love? To "thee" and "thou"? These terms convey great tenderness—but it seems tenderness has become vaguely embarrassing in the age of the superman and the will to power.

The antipathy to love seen in the superman is nothing new. In fact it is characteristic of all identities rooted in the love of resistance. Plato, the patriarch of the sect, found it necessary to discount love as a product of generation—a lesser god compared to the Highest Good of intellect—because love resisted his ideal of pure resistance. The notion that "the good" is pure intellect, pure resistance, requires the negation of all existent values. Love resists this seeming state of purity by continually drawing the philosopher back to the goodness of nature; thus it is necessary to supercede love in order to obtain the good of happiness, according to Plato.

Rationalism produced the same effect, although inadvertently. Descartes used the acid force of resistance furnished by the cogito—pure Subject—to combat Scholasticism and its constructs of Subject and Object. But then the cogito devalued love in three ways. First, the cogito itself is a solipsism—there is nothing romantic about pure Subject. Second, the acidity of the cogito is inimical to tenderness. The cogito glorifies intellect and its critical power at the expense of all other values. And finally the cogito annihilated a way of looking at existence that glorified love. The Schoolmen were looking for the eternal qualities of God in nature; and since the text says God is love, they were inclined to read love into nature's causes and effects. To them, the universe itself was infused with divine love. The cogito destroyed this enchanted view of nature by equating transcendent being with intellect and its force of critical resistance.

The cogito helped to dissolve the hold of "thee" and "thou" on the psyche by introducing a clinical, hypercritical tone into philosophy. Its tough-mindedness can be seen in the anti-romantic spirit of the Enlightenment, the age of satire, and such writers as Swift, Pope and Voltaire. The most influential novel of the age was *Tristram Shandy*, which made a shambles of love by linking the fate of its triste hero to the inopportune thought of an unwound clock on the part of his father just at the moment of generation. The winding of the clock intrudes into the act of love and deprives it of the halo of tenderness it obtains in the romantic imagination.

This *interruptus ratione* was the cause of great hilarity in Sterne as well as in such soul-fellows as Smollet and Fielding, all followers of the divine Cervantes. In sum, the cogito was not overly friendly to love. It did not destroy the language of love because of Descartes' devotion to transcendent being. Descartes saw science as the pursuit of knowledge of a beloved Thou, which notion left room for the tenderness and love of sentiment that are very much on display in *Tristram*. But the cogito does seem to have launched the modern era along a trajectory that diverged increasingly from the view of the universe as a manifestation of divine love. The tenderness of the Schoolmen's teleological synthesis was supplanted by a hard-headed enthusiasm for science and reason for their own sake. Shakespeare's fairies and flowers were chased away by grave-looking men in lab coats.

Kant contributed to the demise of thee and thou by "setting aside" the transcendent. Ironically he was trying to do just the opposite—he was trying restore the Thou to philosophy. Rationalism leads to nothingness by totalizing the force of resistance found in intellect; and nothingness, which is the absence of being, can lead to outright skepticism, as seen in Hume—to the negation of the Thou and an attempt to seek happiness in reason for its own sake. Kant recognized that the cogito caused this nothingness because of the direct link described by Descartes between intellect and transcendent being. It is impossible to use intellect to discover the nature of transcendent being in any direct way for the simple reason that transcendent being is transcendent. But Kant had the clever idea that philosophers could overcome this difficulty by "setting aside" any direct invocation of the transcendent and looking instead for signs of transcendent being in our concepts of value.

Kant deliberately set aside transcendent being in an attempt to reintroduce it in a new form—for instance, as the limit imposed on observational science by time and space. The notion of setting aside transcendent being was clever in two ways. It enabled him to appear to have overcome the nothingness caused by the cogito, the absence of any substantive value judgments about "being," and it also made his method seem more scientific than Scholasticism, more in tune with the spirit of the age. But it resulted in a loss of the inherent tenderness of Scholasticism and its devotion to a beloved Thou. There is nothing tenderhearted about science per se. Kant's admirers were able to salvage some tenderness from Transcendentalism by taking it one step further than he himself was willing to go—by using it to justify their love of nature. This love leaves room for the glowing appreciation of nature seen in Wordsworth and Keats, the belief that nature reflects a tenderhearted Thou, which is why those poets were able to use such terms as "thee" and "thou" without embarrassment.

But Transcendentalism for its own sake led to results that were far from tender. The Transcendental Aesthetic requires the philosopher-scientist to justify himself through scientific method. Just as chemistry experiments must be performed in a meticulous manner in order to justify their conclusions, so Kant reasoned in a measured way in order to make it seem that it was possible to identify middle terms between Rationalism and Empiricism. The synthetic method is rather cool to begin with—its coolness is one of the attributes that distinguishes it from Idealism and the nothingness that results from its fiery force of resistance; but Transcendentalism exacerbated this coolness by setting aside the beloved Thou and focusing on science for its own sake.

This coolness became a little too evident in Hegel, who attempted to go beyond Kant's theoretical superstructure and describe a "scientific synthesis" of being and nothingness. Hegel justified his claim to scientific status by describing intellectual history in evolutionary terms. He set aside the glowing notion of transcendent being seen in Scholasticism and substituted the "Absolute Idea" for the tenderhearted God of the text. Then he tapped into the notion of evolution that was gathering force in his day by claiming that intellectual history was rising to a higher understanding of transcendent being through the dialectical process of positing theses about being and resisting the limitations of those theses through intellect and its critical force of resistance.

Hegel claimed to be able to go beyond the limitations of all previous constructs of being specifically by mediating between them and the nothingness found in intellect and its resistance to their limitations; by attempting to identify nothingness as a limit to those concepts and not as the unrestricted power seen in Rationalism. This heroic effort led to a ratio of value that seemed cold and indifferent on many levels. For one thing, it was difficult to understand. The same ingenuity that gave Hegel the seeming power to analyze that which is evanescent—the transcendent value indicated by our own resistance to the limitations of existent valuations—also caused his analysis to reflect nothingness itself and its resistance to any concept of "being." Also the Absolute Idea seemed monolithically cold and unapproachable. Hegel's eagerness to sprinkle the cool waters of reason on the fiery resistance of the cogito led to the loss of the very fieriness that makes philosophy seem attractive—its resistance to the unhappiness of existence.

That resistance resurfaced in the superman. The coldness of Hegel's attempt to synthesize nothingness with being provided Nietzsche with an opening to seize upon the power of nothingness itself in an attempt to restore the fiery quality of resistance to philosophy. The superman is based on the notion that it is possible to obtain a transcendent identity by using the very nothingness of Hegel's ratio of being and nothingness to negate transcendent being and go beyond the dividedness of philosophy. Nietzsche justified this claim through Darwin's antithetical description of evolution, which made it seem that nature was rising to transcendent value of its own accord through the survival of the fittest.

Darwinism was translated into the will to dominate—a concept that leaves no room for tenderness at all. According to Nietzsche, not only is there no such thing as transcendent being, but the Thou of transcendent being makes men unhappy by causing them to devalue their own existence. Supposedly the way to overcome this unhappiness was to negate the Thou and embrace the will to power. The Thou imposes unnatural restraints on men, according to Nietzsche, by causing them to give up the will to power for such weakling values as pity and kindness—to give up the possibility of obtaining power and accept an unnatural yoke of meekness. And the way out of the predicament was to throw off that yoke by negating the Thou and embracing the natural desire for power.

The theory of value seen in Nihilism annihilates the tenderness of the Thou, first by negating the Thou itself, and then by embracing the will to dominate. Just as the savage satirical spirit of the Enlightenment reflected Rationalism and its resistance to the enchanted universe of the Schoolmen, so the absence of tenderness in the superman reflects Nihilism and the concept that the will to dominate is capable of producing a transcendent identity. Modern literature is characterized by the hard edge of resistance to the good—but this identity imposes a limit on its pleasures and prevents the superman from obtaining the transcendence he desired. The excessive love of intellect seen in philosophy does not lead to the annihilation of tenderness when it is rooted in transcendent Thou; but after the negation of "being," intellect and resistance become philosophy's highest values for their own sake—and there is no tenderness in intellect and its critical power per se.

Nihilism annihilates the tenderness of the Thou and the language of love. No great love stories were written by Modernists, just as there were none in the Enlightenment—and for the same reason. A love of pure resistance is at odds with the tenderness of love. Our modern Ulysses bursts the unnatural constraints of the drawing room and consummates his epic journey in a brothel. No longer does his happiness depend on returning to Penelope; in the modern retelling, Penelope is serially unfaithful, at least in her mind, and the only way her wily lover can find freedom from the entrapments of a palsied domesticity is by making his way to Circe, where Telemachus awaits their mystical reunion.

There can be no question that *Ulysses* is uproarious and entertaining, perhaps the greatest book of its kind since *Don Quixote*, but it reflects the modern ideal of absolute resistance to the good, which is a self-limiting identity. The Transcendental Idealism of the Victorian drawing room may be a sham, but it is impossible to obtain a transcendent identity by attempting to annihilate the drawing room's domestic pleasures for the sake of the brothel. Those pleasures cannot be annihilated by the uproariousness of Circe because they are real. Indeed, the argument can be made that they are more real than Circe, where the false front of salesmanship is inherent in the nature of the transaction.

Now that the smoke has cleared from the great conflagration of Nihilism, it has become possible to "cast a cold eye" on the superman and his pleasures and determine whether they really do have the power to provide happiness. The Circe scene obtains literary value through its sheer force of resistance to Victorianism, which put a high value on fidelity and sexual purity, as well as through the seeming exuberance of its pleasures compared to domestic pleasures. But is Circe really as uproarious as our author makes it seem? Or has his enthusiasm for Nihilism caused him to sentimentalize the brothel, just as Plato sentimentalized Socrates and Sterne sentimentalized Uncle Toby?

Cultural identities rooted in the love of resistance lend themselves to sentimentality by annihilating that which is real. But there is a very significant difference between the love of sentiment on display in Uncle Toby and what is seen in Circe. The love of sentiment characteristic of the Enlightenment reflects the tenderness of a beloved Thou. There was great sweetness in it, and this sweetness leavens the unrelenting hilarity of Sterne's antithetical narration. But this sweetness disappears entirely in the superman after the negation of the Thou. The notion that Circe is a place of transcendent hilarity is sentimental, but there is no trace of Uncle Toby's sweetness in it. Sentiment in the Modern age is devoid of the sweetness of the Thou.

And this is precisely why the superman cannot obtain the domination he so desperately desires—the domination that Joyce claimed for himself.

The Modern age cannot supercede the literary pleasures of the past because it destroys the language of love; it annihilates the tenderness of the Thou and the great sweetness that this tenderness supplies. Circe is the antithesis of Uncle Toby as well as Mr. Woodhouse—but it is impossible to obtain transcendent literary value by annihilating the tenderness of those great portraits because tenderness is a real value in existence. The antiseptic quality of the Modern age and its resistance to the language of love is *different* from the Romanticism of the Transcendentalists and the enchanted view of nature on display in the *Midsummer Night's Dream*. But it cannot obtain domination by attempting to substitute the sentimentality of the Circe episode for the very real sweetness of those other identities.

The superman is capable of obtaining a purer state of resistance than was seen in Rationalism by negating the Thou of "being"—but this purity comes at a high price. It is not possible for Bloom to think of Molly in the tender terms that Homer's Greek warriors think of their wives when his author depicts her as a moll in order to exhibit his resistance to Victorian prudery. The best he can hope for is to obtain some level of emotional release in the mystical same-sex reunion with Stephen in Circe. But then the underlying problem with the love of resistance on display in Circe is that it is sterile. Bloom's relationship with Stephen has the same limitations as Socrates' starry-eyed description of the supposed sublimating potential of pederasty. It does not bring forth life or anything of substance. All that it produces is sentiment.

Free to Play?

NIETZSCHE PAINTED two pictures of the good things that might ensue upon the negation of "the good." One was the superman, who breaks through the dividedness of good and evil to produce "new gods and new ideals." And the other was the transcendent playfulness seen in Dionysus, who romps uninhibited in the Elysian fields.

The superman dominated the early phase of Modernism. It was believed that negating the good would lead to a dramatic breakthrough in consciousness and a transcendent phase of history. But the superman became bogged down in this effort by his own ideal of absolute resistance to the good. He could not overcome the appeal of Hegel's "superior man" without negating the goodness of the sensuous universe that was celebrated in Romanticism—and that goodness stubbornly refused to be negated. The frustration caused by his inability to break through and discover a new realm of existence was reflected in Existentialism, a bleak form of Nihilism that sucked most of the appeal out of the superman by depriving him of transcendent pleasure. He trickled out to nothingness as it began to seem that his will to dominate would lead to a rather grim existence and not the happiness that Nietzsche promised.

But Nihilism and its ideal of absolute resistance was not dead—there was still the possibility of Dionysian play. The first time Nietzsche raised the issue of Dionysus and Apollo he appeared to be echoing Hegel; he seemed to imply that it was desirable to seek a middle term between these extremes. But it became clear later on that Nihilism was dialectical in the Platonic sense. Hegelian "being" was regarded as an Apollonian construct that led to unhappiness by dividing the mind between being and nothingness, while Nihilism was supposed to produce the exuberance seen in Dionysus by grasping nothingness itself and negating that dividedness.

Playfulness is characteristic of the philosophers who follow Plato and his love of the potential of intellect to resist constructs of value. Socrates was the archetype of the playful philosopher, running rings around his plodding interlocutors with their feet stuck in the heavy matter of existence. Hegel described Idealism as a manifestation of the "unhappy consciousness"; by this reckoning, the desire for play might reflect a need to escape from reality. A more charitable appraisal would be that there is a desire for play and a desire for work in the human spirit, and in Socrates the former was ascendant. Certainly there can be no question that Socrates' playfulness is highly appealing and accounts for much of the popularity of Idealism. He believed "the good" was pure intellect. He also believed that the sensuous universe was a mixture of intellect—of the forms of value provided by the transcendent intellect out of the abundance of its goodness—and the dross of matter, in which there is no intrinsic value at all. Thus it seemed to him that it was possible to obtain knowledge of the good by simply negating this unhappy mixture and ascending to the airy regions of pure reason.

Socrates' love of pure intellect and its power to resist sense-based constructs of value reflects something real in human nature because those constructs tend to be convoluted and difficult. If we assume, as the philosophers did, that the essence of the good is intellect, then we also find it necessary to assume that the goodness seen in the sensuous universe is some sort of combination of intellect and matter. But then the problem with making value judgments based on sense is that intellect is nothing like sensuous objects. The qualitative force of resistance that provides intellect with its power to judge cannot be found in those objects as themselves. Therefore the only way to read that qualitative resistance into the sense realm is to create some sort of construct of intellect and matter.

Unfortunately as soon as any attempt is made to develop such a construct philosophy loses the lightness intimated in the good. Constructs of intellect and sense are cumbersome. In order to make such a construct seem realistic it is necessary to carefully define matter so that it seems somehow already to imply the goodness of intellect and to carefully define intellect so that the difference between it and matter is not quite so obvious. This is tedious, difficult work, both for the philosopher who does it and for the student who attempts to absorb it. And there is another limitation to the appeal of constructive methods: after the philosopher is done with all of that hard work, he is still mired in the same old existence that made him unhappy in the first place. The constructive method is rooted in the goodness of the sensuous universe, but then it deprives the philosopher of the freedom to imagine something better than that which already exists.

To Socrates, the solution seemed simple. It was not necessary to weary one's eternal spirit with the syllogisms and middle terms of synthetic methods. All the philosopher had to do to transcend the unhappiness of existence was to negate the mixture of intellect and matter he thought he saw in the sense realm and embrace the freedom of pure intellect. But in actual practice his love of pure intellect introduces a characteristic problem into philosophy. If the good is the same thing as the force of resistance to existence experienced in unhappiness, then the only way to obtain knowledge of the good is to totalize that resistance and negate all existent values. And this negation leads to nothingness. By negating embodied values, Idealism prevents the playful philosopher from putting meat on the bones of his concept of the good of happiness.

All of those who follow Socrates and his love of pure intellect wind up having the same limitation as Idealism in the end because pure resistance always leads to pure negation. The antithetical method with its promise of simplicity and freedom from constructs of value can be made to sound highly appealing by capable propagandists like Socrates or Descartes—as long as it remains nothing more than a theory of value—but its limitations become obvious as soon as any attempt is made to put it into effect. Pure resistance cannot lead to any substantive concept of value of its own accord. And an ironic effect of the method is that it deprives the philosopher of the very freedom he desires in the end. If we follow Socrates' way of thinking, existence is literally made up of form and matter. The negation of matter, then, leaves pure form, a rigid value, as seen in the totalitarian *Republic* and repressive *Laws*.

Socrates' love of playfulness is the same thing that is seen in Postmodernism and its preoccupation with "play." Postmodernism is a rearguard action of Nietzsche and Nihilism, but it is not always appreciated how similar Nihilism is to Idealism. Nihilism appears to be the opposite of Idealism because Plato based his philosophy on the pursuit of the good and Nihilism is based on the negation of the good; but like Idealism, Nihilism reflects a desire for freedom from a construct of value—in this case, the Transcendental Aesthetic; and like Idealism, Nihilism discloses a desire for simple, absolute values—the will to dominate and "pure existence" from which any trace of the good has been expunged; and like Idealism, Nihilism leads to the negation of all existent values, since nothing can be good if the good quite literally does not exist. Finally, Nihilism leads to totalitarian values, as does Idealism, by using pure nothingness to negate Hegel's construct of nothingness and being.

Unlike Idealism, however, Nihilism negates the good and the possibility it implies of going beyond the limitations of existence. Indeed, it attempts to obtain transcendence specifically by embracing that existence. The premise of Nihilism is that there are transcendent principles in human existence for its own sake—specifically the will to power. According to Nietzsche, it is possible to obtain the status of a superman by negating any thought of the good and embracing that potentially transcendent principle within. But of course there is nothing very playful about the will to dominate others. Nihilism in its early phase—the phase of the super-man—was compelled to give up the playfulness that resistance affords for the sake of the will to power.

The death of the superman rings in the rearguard action known as Postmodernism. This second-phase Nihilism is far more playful than the superman because it is based on Dionysus, party deity supreme. But its natural limitation is that there is nothing very playful about existence for its own sake—about pure sense devoid of intellect and its capacity for resistance. By negating the good and the presumed difference between this value and existence, Postmodernism negates the play that this difference afforded to Socrates. The philosopher must attempt to identify some value in sensuous existence per se that is playful, and the only such value that readily presents itself to the imagination is sex and its potential resistance to normative conventions; to Victorianism and other repressive manifestations of transcendentalism. But while sex can certainly be playful, its playfulness is a limited value. It is not as much fun or playful in an intellectual sense as Socrates or Descartes and their high-flying resistance to synthetic metaphysics.

The seriousness with which Postmodern philosophers attempt to make sex seem incandescently playful can lead to humorous results—but not necessarily for the reasons they intend. Roland Barthes, for instance, would have his readers believe that the modern ideal of absolute resistance to the good has the power to produce *jouissance*, apparently an ecstatic state of existence which is available to enlightened cultural critics like himself who are willing to go beyond good and evil. Now it is safe to say that ecstasy and criticism were not often uttered in the same breath before Barthes. The tradition of criticism that developed in the wake of Hegel was careful and deliberate and sought to illuminate texts by establishing historical contexts. Such a method did not lend itself to playfulness, especially since it was based on the assumption that historical reality is fixed.

Jouissance is intended as the antithesis to those historical labors. It is described as a form of pure erotic play that can be obtained in the act of criticism (and, presumably, by reading such criticism). *Jouissance* is a neologism based on Eros. It reflects Freud and the notion that all of human existence is erotic in essence. According to this view, there is no such thing as the good, and therefore intellect does not reflect some ethereal being that does not have a body. Instead intellect and body are a monism energized by sex. This concept of existence makes it seem possible to totalize mind and body in intellectual activities of a sexual nature; to annihilate the dividedness of philosophy between intellect and sense and obtain transcendent value. By bravely grasping *jouissance* and its resistance to all forms of transcendentalism, the critic appears to obtain the power to experience criticism as a totalizing erotic pleasure.

Like Socrates, all of this may sound quite promising in theory. The deconstructive power of pure resistance produces a thrill by negating the unhappiness of existing constructs of value—in this case an erotic thrill. But the limitation of all methods of describing value rooted in pure resistance is that they rapidly lose their appeal as soon as they make any attempt to reenter existence. Resistance can provide a thrill in itself—but the same thing that makes it seem thrilling also divides it from substantive values. Socrates' playfulness and talk about the happiness of pure intellect sound highly appealing until he attempts to go beyond resistance and describe the effects of Idealism in real existence, as in the Republic, which is not playful in any degree. At that point the rigidity of resistance and form comes into view and exposes the limitations of Idealism compared with the goodness of sensuous values.

The same problem is seen in Postmodernism. The limitations of its love of pure resistance become evident as soon as it attempts to go beyond the theory of Nihilism and actually show its results. *Jouissance* has a good deal of pleasurable resonance as long as it remains in the realm of pure resistance—but the attempt to wring totalized pleasure from the act of criticism produces limited results for the very reason that *jouissance* is predicated on Eros. *Jouissance* annihilates all context and reduces existence to the single unifying theory that sex must be lurking somewhere at the core of all forms of communication. But then the very thing that makes *jouissance* seem potent—its capacity to totalize value—is also its weakness, since Eros is a limited way of looking at the value of "texts."

The advantage of Freudian and Marxist methods of interpreting literature is that these are unifying theories and can be applied universally. It is quite possible to retrofit every speech in Shakespeare into a Freudian framework because the theory is just vague enough and just plausible enough to be beyond falsification. No one can prove beyond a shadow of a doubt that a Freudian reading of Shakespeare is false; certainly is it *possible* that all of human existence is sexual in essence, since there can be no doubt that humans are sexual beings and sex is highly desirable. This possibility provides the strength of the method. But its corresponding weakness is that it excludes—even prohibits—any interpretations that are *not* sexual in nature. It attempts to use Eros to liberate the critic and philosopher from existing constructs of value, but because of the totalitarian nature of theory it enslaves them to one single, narrow concept of value.

So it is with *jouissance*. Its power is found in its capacity to unify experience and simplify the act of criticism—but simplifying criticism for the sake of Eros imposes an unnecessary limitation on its pleasures. *Jouissance* appears to provide the master key to all knowledge and value, but the door that it opens leads to a narrow closet. It imposes the same type of rigidity on value judgments that was seen in Idealism by insisting on one unifying principle—that all value is intrinsically sexual. *Jouissance* intimates a force of pure resistance to the limitations of existing approaches to criticism, but pure resistance is not an unlimited value in itself. It has the same self-limiting effect in *jouissance* as in Idealism: it leads to nothingness. Barthes' theory of value provides greater pleasure as a theory than it does when he attempts to put it into practice because the results of reducing all experience to Eros are limited and highly predictable.

For that matter, it is not certain that Barthes' method of reading is sexual at all. His concept of the value of *jouissance* is based on a particular worldview, a story about value called Modernism, but there is no reason to assume that this story is any more valid than Plato and his notion that all of reality was intellectual in nature. The great pleasure Barthes claims to receive from deconstructing the texts of popular culture comes from intellect and its capacity for resistance, but this resistance is not sexual per se. There is nothing inherently sexual about it. The very notion that intellect is sexual in nature reveals the difference between intellect and Eros, since there are no ideas in sex for its own sake. Sex has no quality of resistance, as Darwin was forced to concede with the failure of cultivated breeds to retain their beautiful forms when left to their own devices. Indeed, sex might almost be called a force of pure attraction.

Just as Plato and his fellow philosophers were unable to obtain happiness by negating sense for the sake of pure intellect, so Barthes was unable to produce *jouissance* by totalizing the pleasures of Eros at the expense of intellect and its capacity for resistance to sense. There is a great if uneasy pleasure in seeing Hector vacillate between his fury at his brother's fecklessness and the affection stirred by his endearing qualities. Whenever Hector tries to summon the thunderbolts of judgment, he finds himself disarmed by Paris's capacity for self-deprecation and readiness to concur. Through his unwillingness to condemn Paris, Hector puts himself in great danger—but he also rises to a value in the mind of the reader that Paris cannot attain. The erotic pleasure of having Helen and the pleasure provided by Hector's magnanimity are two different things. By eroticizing the text, *jouissance* annihilates a great and subtle literary pleasure for the sake of a more limited one.

These same limitations are also evident in *differance*, which is a core value of the critical movement known as Deconstruction. Of course there is nothing new about difference per se—it was the difference between intellect and sense that inspired Plato to take up Idealism. But what is different about *differance* is its eroticism. The little *a* that creeps in where it is not expected is not there to exhibit contempt for orthography; it is intended as a sign that *differance* has the power to produce something radically different from Idealism and restore the quality of pure resistance intimated by the *a*, the alpha, to a priori methods. And that something is erotic pleasure. *Differance* has the aura of a naughty boy who negates all plodding constructs of value through a playful sexuality. It luxuriates in sexual metaphor in an effort to induce the "trembling" of a transcendent eroticism. It piques itself on an insouciant resistance to the weight of traditional discourse.

Since Hegel hogged the pages of history with the scientific synthesis and its interminable ratiocinations, Derrida takes up the resistance he spies in the white margin of the printed page and declares his intention to play there. The appeal of this image is found in its power to intimate the pleasures of play as opposed to the fatiguing labors of Hegel and historical method—but it also indicates the limitations of play, since the white margin is not the same thing as the text with its pleasures. One can declare one's intention to stay in the margin, but not without forfeiting the rewards that come to those who are willing to labor in the denser text of the middle way. The white margin is pure, but this also means that it contains no matter, no words, which are the substance of literature. To cling to the freedom of the margin from the labor of the text, then, is to deny oneself the opportunity to obtain the pleasures that the text can provide.

To make this somewhat more concrete, one of the great pleasures of reading a classic "text" is to be eased into it by an introduction written by a seasoned scholar who knows intellectual history, knows how to put the work into context, writes with some ease and grace, and has no axe to grind. It is a great labor to read much, digest much, work over one's concepts until they begin to obtain clarity, and be self-effacing enough to keep one's hobbyhorses out of view—but it can be a labor of love. And hard work of this nature has its rewards. There is pleasure in being able to write such an authoritative introduction, just as there is pleasure for the reader who is hungry for context and seeking a reliable guide; who is curious about intellectual history and whose pleasure in reading a given book is enhanced by understanding its context.

The problem with negating all such labor for the sake of pure play is that those labors have literary and intellectual value. If it is true that all work and no play makes Jack a dull boy, then all play and no work makes Jack seem childish. *Differance* can provide pleasure by naughtily resisting the tedious labor of the historical method—but it cannot also satisfy the historical curiosity of the reader. It cannot take up Nihilism and its force of pure resistance as a cudgel against all constructs of value and also produce a seasoned, satisfying introduction to a work of literature. All that *differance* can accomplish as a critical tool is to deconstruct the work in question and expose its presumed limitations. And since it has only one theme—that all value is erotic in nature—such exercises tend to lead to limited results.

For that matter, is *differance* really all that playful? The play of children can provide ecstatic freedom when they forget themselves—but it is impossible for adults to become children again for the very reason that they are adults and conscious of their sexuality. The freedom they are looking for cannot be found in Paris if erotic absolutism is the cause of the Trojan War. But Hector can find freedom in his *love* for his brother, which liberates him from the moral absolutism represented by the steel of Agamemnon as well as his brother's laconic nihilism—which is a larger and more expansive value than either "the good" or erotic love.

Making Paris the hero of the story through the ideal of erotic play negates this complexity and the entanglements of history, but it also negates the emotional engagement that the story invites, especially the tears and pity caused by Hector's all-too foolish demise. *Differance* is like Paris, who in his childish self-absorption would have no freedom or pleasure at all if it were not for Hector and his largesse. Hector does not turn his brother over to his foes; he protects him and his right to be free. But with Hector dead, the good work is undone, and the limitations of erotic play are exposed.

Dame Fortune

LAUGHTER, THEY say, is the best medicine; but lo, the poor superman. He cannot afford to laugh at himself. His religion is his own capacity for power, his ability to obtain a transcendent identity through the will to dominate. When that fails, he has nothing to fall back on but his tears.

Modernism is very serious about itself. It is based on the premise of becoming a superman—a transcendent being—through absolute resistance to the Dominus, "the good" of philosophers and religionists. This identity is obtained by negating the Dominus and embracing the will to dominate; in short, by making oneself into a new dominus. But such an identity deprives the superman of the freedom to laugh at himself. Philosophers can afford self-deprecation when they acknowledge the good and the great difference between this value and themselves. This humble acknowledgement gives them the freedom to smile at their own shortcomings. But it is impossible for the superman to laugh at himself when his identity is predicated on domination. The value judgment he seeks requires a show of power; no acknowledgement of weakness is permitted.

Men were not always afraid of laughing at themselves and their ambitions. In fact there was a time when one of the most cherished figments of the popular imagination was the jolly old Wheel of Fortune, which raised up courtiers to giddy heights only to cast them down again with reckless abandon. The Wheel could be cruel, but there could also be a good deal of self-effacing humor in it because its cruelty was generally regarded as the just consequence of human weakness. The Wheel gave the courtier the comeuppance he deserved for being too ambitious, casting down those who were foolish enough to forsake philosophy. Great men were notoriously fickle, and to fly too close to the sun of their power was to risk getting burned.

The self-effacing humor of the Wheel reflected a consciousness of human shortcomings, especially the love of money and power. The culture of the Middle Ages was devoted to Aristotle and his concept of the golden mean. Just as a salubrious bath should be neither too hot nor too cold, so the philosophic man should avoid extremes in the political realm, neither rising up too high nor staying too low. It was just when the courtier failed to pay attention to this counsel that he became susceptible to Dame Fortune, a seductive goddess, luring men into the pursuit of wealth and fame and then to a fall.

Everyone knew that to woo Fortune was to court disaster. And yet the strange jollity of the Wheel came from a collective consciousness that most men would seek Fortune if they could in spite of this knowledge. The fact that they knew what was prudent and right did not meant that they were inclined to do what was right. Why, even a great philosopher like Boethius was not immune to the Wheel and its charms. Boethius's fall gave the medieval courtier the freedom to laugh at himself and to find a certain macabre humor in his predicament, since it indicated that all men are weak by nature and likely to make fools of themselves, if given the opportunity.

The Wheel was a humane image in the sense that it acknowledged the manifold weaknesses of humanity. Men fall for the same reason Adam fell—because they are vain; because they are ambitious and do not pay attention to their own philosophy; because they follow mammon and not God. The Wheel gave the courtier the freedom to laugh at himself if he was humble enough and sensible enough to accept these foolish facts about himself. But there was something else about the Wheel and the culture it reflected that made it humane. The humor of the Wheel reflected the dedication of the Middle Ages to a gracious God who is willing to overlook the shortcomings of his creatures. In Aristotle the Wheel is cruel and arbitrary; but to the medieval mind, its cruelty was leavened by a belief that this world is not all there is; that those who fall can be lifted up in a new way and find a happiness the world cannot give.

This was the "fortunate fall," or *felix culpa*, as the monks called it. According to this complex and counterintuitive theory of value, there can be a strange kind of happiness in being cast down by the physics of the Wheel—because only then does one obtain the great privilege of being raised up by a gracious and all-powerful creator. Only when one is compelled to see one's weakness and insufficiency does it become possible to truly taste the sweetness of a merciful God, the same God who is said to bring down the high and mighty and lift up the lowly; who fills the hungry with good things while the rich are sent away empty. This is a radical message, a soulful gospel, and it was delectable food for an age when man's other possibilities seemed distinctly limited.

The Wheel of Fortune obtained metaphorical power through the economic situation in which the courtier found himself. Europe had long since been carved up into the great estates, feudal or ecclesiastical, and so the handiest way for an ambitious courtier to improve his lot was to rise in the estimation of an autocratic overlord. The Wheel was a product of economic stasis—it provided a way to rise without actually moving forward. The courtier who was willing to avail himself of its upward physics could leapfrog those who were in his way and ascend directly into the favor of the overlord; but autocrats can be fickle, and to rise too high was to invite a rapid descent on the sunset side. Also human nature is not pleased to feel the imprint of someone else's foot upon its neck. Thus the rising motion of the Wheel produced a combustible combination of putting oneself too much into the glare of one's overlord and too much in the envy of one's fellow climbers.

To be good, in the mind of the medieval courtier, was to love God and one's neighbors as oneself; and since the fastest way to rise up on the Wheel was to break both commandments at once, the comeuppance that came to fortune's darlings often seemed well-deserved. The self-deprecating humor of the Wheel reflected the high value that was assigned to humility in that distant culture, which in turn reflected the reality of everyday life. Most courtiers had no hope of becoming overlords and had to accommodate themselves to servitude. Their world seemed constricted, especially with the expansion of the Ottoman Empire, which pressed upon the borders of Europe. For that matter, life itself was tenuous, with no protection against infection and poor nutrition and sanitation. A man was considered fortunate to live to the ripe, old age of sixty at a time when multitudes might be consumed by recurring plagues.

This love of humility faded, however, as several factors converged to produce a more hopeful view of human potential and possibility. Prominent among these were the rise of the new learning and the scientific revolution. One change that marked the difference between the Middle Ages and the modern era was the growing belief that science had the power to bring happiness to the human race; that man's destiny was in his own hands and not in the stars. Other fundamental changes included the emergence of capitalism and discovery of the New World. No longer was it necessary to seek fortune in the good graces of an overlord when one could become rich through commerce. And everything that seemed cramped and limited in the old imagination simply melted away as the good news of Columbus's discovery spread through Europe. The New World represented an opportunity to escape the tyranny of Dame Fortune and make one's own fortune by obtaining land and the freedom to benefit directly from one's labors.

All of these factors converged to obliterate Dame Fortune from the collective consciousness and cause men to forget Boethius and the fortunate fall. Something entirely new was born—the self-made man who forged his own happiness. The enthusiasm for science led to important improvements that helped to liberate humankind from the stench of death. Capitalism began to generate wealth not just for the capitalists but for the working class as well. In Jefferson's time over ninety percent of Americans lived on farms, but they began to flee the farm for the factory and hard cash as industrial capitalism became the prevalent generator of wealth. And as they did, capitalism continued to drive down the middle term of price, raising them up into the middle class.

The modern era is, in a material sense, incomparably preferable to the Middle Ages. There is far more economic freedom and opportunity. Modern man is far healthier and lives more than twice as long as his medieval counterpart. There is an abundance of fresh, wholesome food, as well as antibiotics and other life-saving medicines. Technology makes work easy and facilitates travel and unlimited entertainment. And the average citizen of a modern Western society is far richer in material things than any but the richest courtier. Man has risen to a pinnacle never before seen in history through science, technology and capitalism.

But one consequence of his apotheosis was a loss of the graciousness seen in the Wheel of Fortune and the notion of the fortunate fall. These things passed from the modern psyche because men believed in their power to obtain happiness and justify their existence. The heroic notion of the self-made man pushed the Supreme Being out of philosophy and suppressed collective consciousness of the difference between its goodness and human existence. The superman cannot laugh at himself because he has negated God and turned himself into a "new God." He must appear to be powerful at all times, to be invincible, and this imperative deprives him of the aura of graciousness that characterized the Middle Ages and its consciousness of its own limitations.

There are signs that those limitations may now be coming back into view, however. The modern experiment failed to produce the "new Gods and new ideals" promised by Nietzsche. The superman was unable to obtain the dominance he desired because his love of pure resistance led to nothingness, as seen in Modern culture and the arts. And his failure to transcend the limitations of philosophy indicates the end of the modern age and the attempt to obtain happiness through mortal means. Philosophy was the pursuit of the good of happiness, but Nihilism is predicated on the idea that happiness can be obtained through the negation of the good;

thus philosophy loses the ability to promise happiness as the limitations of Nihilism come into view.

Meanwhile it seems that the limitations of human existence are becoming more obvious again on the economic front as well. Capitalism may now be approaching a limit to its capacity to generate wealth. The synergy of capitalism and industrialism depends to a large degree upon cheap labor and energy; as the costs of production increase, capitalism loses its aura of unlimited possibility. The strategy of driving down the middle term of price through manufacturing and distribution efficiencies is also self-limiting. When all of those efficiencies have been realized, the only way to perpetuate the illusion of unlimited wealth is through credit, which leads to a net decrease in buying power.

Also, by a strange irony, the dream of unlimited wealth generation produced by modern capitalism appears to be leading to a new feudalism—an oligarchy in which the middle class binds itself by golden handcuffs to corporate overlords. The same consolidation process that makes capitalism powerful also leads to a loss of individualism. Family businesses succumb to superstores and chains that use massive buying power to manipulate price. The market and its middle term are carved up by mega-corporations that dominate manufacturing, mega-banks that control the money supply, giant retail chains that dominate merchandising. The feudal estate reemerges as the corporate estate, with its campuses and wire fences and security details.

As a result, the middle class becomes a corporate courtier class whose well-being depends on the good graces of vassals. Corporate courtiers curry the favor of an autocratic overlord in order to rise; but the higher they rise, the more precarious their position becomes, especially as the middle term of capitalism becomes increasingly unstable through debt accumulation and increasing energy and labor costs. The Wheel of Fortune, with its stasis-oriented physics, begins to return as a fact of life, if not as a figment of the popular imagination. Unlike his ancient counterpart, however, the corporate courtier does not have the consolation of philosophy to leaven his thankless existence.

The modern age is the most fortunate age and also the saddest age. We abandoned the middle way of life and imagined ourselves to be supermen because capitalism appeared to be capable of generating unlimited wealth; we abandoned the gracious, self-deprecating humor of the Wheel for the vanity of the self-made man and the notion that humankind was capable of making itself happy. Thus we have nothing to redeem us when we fall. There is no *fortunate* fall for modern man. Fortuna returns with all of the cold indifference of the Pagan goddess, unsmiling and unrepentantly cruel.

Why Shakespeare Was
Not a Christian

PROFESSOR BLOOM claims to see no sign that Shakespeare was a Christian. In one sense this assertion may seem odd, since Shakespeare is full of Christian tropes, which routinely find their way into the mouths of even non-Christian characters, and since he declared himself to be "hoping and assuredly believing through the only merits of Jesus Christ my Saviour to be made partaker of life everlasting." But in another sense the assertion is perfectly correct—because there is a type of Christianity that quite literally cannot be seen.

In short, there are two types of "Christianity." There is the institution that seeks power in the world and can take forms as disparate as bishops in their regalia, television evangelists, seminaries, publishing houses, record companies, local churches clinging to various forms of sectarianism, and political action committees. This type of Christianity can be conventional, defensive, smug, full of small judgments. But there is another type of Christianity that is said to be "not of this world" and to have "no place to lay its head." This type of Christianity is open, generous, forgiving, free. It is not triumphal. It does not seek precedence within existing power structures—in fact it tends to be subversive. And because of this it is also sometimes tragic.

The first type of Christianity is the one that is more readily "seen," since it actively seeks power and influence in the world. Shakespeare represented it in such characters as Cardinal Pandulph, who comes in state to set France against the apostate island, blithely stirring up war with no apparent concern for justice as he seeks to protect the financial interests of the church. But the second type has no use for outward signs of power because its "kingdom is not of this world." There is no intrinsic relation between this hidden type of Christianity and the vestments, buildings, rituals, doctrines, and other trappings of the institutional church. Indeed, it is just as likely to be defined through resistance to the soullessness of such things.

This resistance is naturally subversive to the existing order. The crucifixion was a new kind of tragedy—a man is killed for being too kind. The religious leaders wanted him out of the way because his graciousness posed a threat to their stranglehold on the sheep. They were offended when sins were forgiven and burdens relieved because their cachet depended on controlling the rituals of purification; offended to see a man healed on the Sabbath because they derived their claim to holiness from the law, which they did not understand on account of their vanity; offended to hear him call himself the son of God because the messiah they were looking for was an earthly king with worldly power who would make them his lieutenants.

The cross was a highly subversive sign of power because it showed that the power of God and the power of this world are two different things. Caesar sits on his imperial throne; the Sanhedrin has its gilded corridors and vestments; the king of love dies naked and broken. The cross was an offense to the world, a scandal. It was offensive to the philosophers because they wanted to glorify intellect and its power to provide happiness, and by the measure of intellect the cross appears to be complete foolishness. It was an offense to "the Jews" because of its nakedness. They thought they could clothe themselves in good works, but the cross exposed their vanity.

The offensiveness of the cross cannot be separated from its soulfulness. The story of the Prodigal Son is soulful because of the father's gracious love but also because of the resistance of this graciousness to the limitations of the mortal realm, as represented by the older brother and his resentment—the resistance of life, which is a spiritual value, to the natural love of judgment, which is rooted in death and fear of the grave. This resistance is also seen in the reaction of the Pharisee to the sinful woman who came and began to wash the feet of her master with her tears. Simon's judgment was correct: she had behaved sinfully in the past. He had status in definition to her which he was unwilling to relinquish; he was unwilling to let go of the power of judgment, which is narrow and brings bitterness, for the sake of the gracious value of life.

To follow the way of the cross is to seek identity in mercy and resist the temptation to use judgment to make oneself seem more important than one's fellow beings. To "take up the cross" is to suffer, since it requires giving up everything in human nature that cries out for distinction; and this suffering can obtain tragic dimensions, especially when the bearer is worthy of distinction. The physical pain of the cross may not have been more difficult to endure than the psychological pain of being despised and rejected, especially by those who identified themselves as the religious authorities. And the command to take up his cross and follow him suggests that anyone who seeks identity in the sign of love must be willing to endure a similar type of suffering; to be "treated as an imposter, and yet true; as unknown, and yet well-known."

Those who seek identity in the soulfulness of the cross are like "strangers and aliens" in the world because the power of the cross is encoded. Alienation causes suffering—and yet the same force of resistance that produces their alien status also provides them with a secret wisdom that the world does not share. They are blessed in the sense that they experience the soulfulness of the cross and the great love it demonstrates, which cannot be found in the world. They are also blessed in the sense that they obtain wisdom about what is "good" that goes far beyond anything found in philosophy. And since their concept of value is informed by the humility and gentleness of the cross, they obtain special insight into human behavior. They see the world and its vanity for what they are. They revel in the difference between the cross and the world.

Now it is true, to return for a moment to Professor Bloom, that there is little evidence in Shakespeare of the type of Christianity that seeks power in the world—Pandulph Christianity. Shakespeare was not a "Christian" author in the sense that Dante or Spenser or Milton might be considered Christian authors—authors in whom Christianity takes an outward form. He was not an apologist and made no attempt to use his rhetorical powers to procure a more prominent place for Christianity in the world. But this does not mean there is no sign of the encoded power of the cross in Shakespeare. Quite the contrary—the case can be made that it is impossible to understand him apart from the sign of love and its soulful resistance to the world.

It would not be difficult to demonstrate fealty to Christianity through linear analysis of Shakespeare's plays, since there are allusions in almost every major speech either to the faith itself or the worldview it produces—even in characters in whom such allusions seem absurd, as Dr. Johnson noted. But Shakespeare's devotion to the soulfulness of the cross goes far deeper than these outward manifestations. It can be seen, for example, in Cordelia and her determination to "love and be silent." Cordelia is willing to suffer and be misunderstood because love is too sacred to be bartered for land, even for a third of a kingdom. At great cost to herself she chooses the sincerity of a pure love over the temptation to feign love and flatter her father. And her sacrifice is made all the more poignant by the fact that her father would have been content with a very little flattery indeed.

Cordelia's decision to love and be silent reflects the concept that there is no profit in gaining the whole world and losing one's soul. This concept indicates that the soul and the world are in profound conflict. It is possible to follow mammon and gain the whole world but not without giving up the soulfulness of the sign of love. Cordelia cannot do what her father wants her to do and also cling to the purity of the cross and its truthfulness. The cross was naked; nothing was feigned there. It was brutally honest about the human condition and vanity of those who believe they can transcend their fellow mortals through outward signs of power. Love can be feigned for the sake of material gain, but love that is feigned is not sincere. Cordelia cannot cling to the sincerity of the sign of love and also satisfy her father's unreasonable demand.

"Love and be silent" directly echoes a passionate precedent—the silence maintained before Pilate in the face of death. Cordelia's sincere love engenders her father's wrath because it is subversive to his construct of power. He wants to give her the best third of the kingdom because he feels that she loves him best. In addition to his genuine affection for her, he sees her as a bulwark against the ambitions of her sisters. His seemingly generous offer is designed to tempt Cordelia into seeking distinction in the world—but the cross shows that "love is not self-seeking." Lear's temptation is the cause of his own undoing, since it compels him to reward the feigned love of his older daughters. Thus the sincerity of the sign of love and the soulfulness of its resistance to the world are the basis of the play and the key to understanding it.

Professor Bloom is right, then, when he claims to see no *sign* of Christianity in Shakespeare. The soulfulness of Cordelia's choice cannot be outwardly seen and must be understood through a frame of reference that is not alluded to explicitly in the play. And yet it should be noted that the good professor does not seem overly eager to find such a sign. His thesis is that Shakespeare was a superman and not a passionate pilgrim. Professor Bloom is a classical Nihilist who believes in the superman just as Nietzsche described him—the great man who obtains a transcendent identity through domination. The possibility of this transcendent being is the basis of Modernism. But the superman never quite materialized. Modernism propped itself up with bluster and self-congratulation but failed to produce any artist who was capable of obtaining transcendent status.

The failure of Modernism to produce any real supermen led to the rearguard action known as Postmodernism, which attempted to perpetuate Nihilism and its resistance to "the good" by discarding the superman and embracing resistance for its own sake. According to the Postmodernists, it is the very notion of the great man that is an impediment to transcendent value, reflecting the biases of the patriarchy. It is not surprising that the superman should have caused such a backlash, considering Nietzsche's patronizing attitude toward women. But Postmodernism's ideal of pure resistance to the notion of great men and "great books" poses a threat to Professor Bloom and his status as a leading expositor of the Western Canon. If it is true, as the Postmodernists claim, that there are literally no great authors—that the so-called canon is little more a construct of value for the purpose of oppressing women and minorities—then there is no good reason to perpetuate English departments and no ready-made cult for literary gurus like Professor Bloom.

In short, it appears that Professor Bloom wants to make Shakespeare into a superman in order to save his dinner from the harpies of Postmodernism. If Shakespeare was such a man, then Postmodernism is routed and the Western canon preserved. Unfortunately turning Shakespeare into a superman requires a rewriting of intellectual history. The superman is the product of Nihilism and the clever notion that pure nothingness has the power to negate the enervating effects of Hegel's construct of nothingness and being. This notion is the basis of Professor Bloom's claim that there are no signs of Christianity in Shakespeare—he must make the case that Shakespeare embraced Nihilism and its opposition to "the good" in order to make him into a superman. But Nihilism has no historical context apart from Hegel and his construct. There was nothing to be gained by using pure nothingness to annihilate the construct of being and nothingness until that construct came into being and obtained power. The clever strategy Nietzsche used against Hegel would have seemed as foreign to Shakespeare as the Christian concepts he himself loved to put into the mouths of classical heroes.

As already noted, it would not be difficult to compile an extensive list of allusions to Christianity and the Christian worldview in Shakespeare that contradict the notion that he was a superman—that he did not believe in the existence of a transcendent being; that he embraced the notion of absolute resistance to "the good." But a more illuminating way of addressing this claim is to evaluate its impact on Professor Bloom's interpretation of the plays. Interpretation depends upon a theory of value; hence Professor Bloom must make the case that Shakespeare's concept of value is the same as the superman's. And since Nihilism negates the good and all concepts of value that glorify transcendent being, the superman must attempt to justify his claim to transcendent status by glorifying some heroic quality that can be found in himself.

According to Professor Bloom, the superhuman quality glorified in Shakespeare's plays is intellect. In this view, Shakespeare was an intellectual and valued intellect above all things. Now what Shakespeare valued most is not a trivial matter, since this value becomes encoded directly into the action of the plays. Shakespeare's plays have heroes and villains who are in conflict with each other. They keep our interest because we identify with the heroes and their struggles. But how can we tell the heroes and villains apart? What is it about the heroes that identifies them as heroes and is glorified in their struggles? According to Professor Bloom, this supernal quality is intellect. Shakespeare's heroes obtain exalted status because they are more intelligent than their antagonists.

But while characters like Cordelia and Hamlet are certainly intelligent, their appeal is not based on intellect per se. Surely Hamlet was not thinking of a high IQ when he claimed to have "that within which passes show, These but the trappings and the suits of woe." He was referring to the sincerity of his grief and his love for his father. There is no evidence that intellect per se constitutes the difference between Hamlet and Claudius. The king's self-aggrandizing speeches reveal a remarkable talent for seeing into the minds of men and developing rhetorical strategies accordingly, a gift for manipulation and seizing upon the will to dominate that is said to be the superman's path to happiness. In fact the case can be made that it is Claudius, the villain, who more closely resembles the superman in the play.

No, the real difference between Hamlet and Claudius is that Hamlet is soulful. His sincere love for his father separates him from the false regret sounded by Claudius in his self-serving political proclamations. Hamlet appears "not to be" because his grief has deprived him of the desire to act; but his seeming powerlessness for the sake of sincere love is linked to his soulfulness, a different order of power. This soulfulness is subversive, exposing the vanity of the court and Claudius's ambition. Hamlet must be killed in the end because his sincere love for his father makes him a threat to the existing power structure.

The superior intelligence Professor Bloom sees in Hamlet is linked to this same soulfulness. Hamlet has the key to a puzzle that others find perplexing because his grief for his father is real. Even before encountering the Ghost, he can see through Claudius's posturing when he pretends to grieve for his brother because Hamlet knows that true grief robs the tongue of eloquence. He can see through the emissaries that Claudius sends in an effort to neutralize him because his grief has alienated him from politics and attuned him to the machinations of ambition. It is his sincere love that deconstructs the world and its vanity. The honesty of his soulful grief furnishes a natural qualitative resistance to signs of falsity and self-interest in others.

The subversiveness of Hamlet's love indicates the difference between ancient tragedy and the cross. Aristotle identified the "fatal flaw" as the cause of the downfall of tragic heroes because he inhabited a thought-world where good and evil were determined by judgment and appearances of power. If intellect and judgment have the power to determine what is good, then tragic heroes must be fatally flawed in some way in order support the existing order. They must bring their downfall on themselves, or else their tragedy becomes an indictment of that order—the order of judgment—which leads to absurdity. The cross inverts this formulation because it is a judgment on the world. There is an order of value that is not seen in the world, and those who cling to this hidden order may suffer as their soulfulness comes into conflict with the world. Cordelia and Hamlet do not bring their tragedies upon themselves through any specific flaw. Their stories are tragic because their fidelity to sincere love puts them at odds with the world.

It is sincere love that makes them heroic—different from the world—not intellect per se. And in fact it is difficult to think of any characters in Shakespeare who obtain heroic status through intellect for its own sake. Marc Antony outwits Brutus, but he is not the star of the ensuing war—even on his own side. Sir Toby makes a fool of Malvolio, but he is not to be compared with his niece for all of his wit. Falstaff runs verbal rings around Prince Hal, but the new king makes a point of putting all tomfoolery behind him when confronted with the seriousness of his charge. Meanwhile there are many appealing characters in Shakespeare who are shown in distinctly anti-intellectual colors. Kent is a blunt fellow who is honest and faithful, who hates injustice and knows true worth when he sees it. Gonzalo, Adam and Enobarbus are also in this straightforward vein. Horatio is a faithful friend who exhibits none of the subtlety of Rosencrantz and Guildenstern. Antonio seems downright foolish, judged by business sense. Is it intellect that accounts for the difference between Prospero and his brother? For that matter, if intellect is the measure of value, then what are we to make of Miranda and Ferdinand?

Meanwhile Shakespeare's most self-consciously intellectual character also happens to be one of the most foolish—Jacques, the significance of whose sign cannot be mistaken, since his author takes the extraordinary measure of having it illuminated. Some insight into Shakespeare's attitude toward intellect per se may be gleaned from the way he frames the famous "seven ages of man" speech. This threnody is still ringing in the ears of the audience when Orlando comes in bearing faithful old Adam in his arms, who is far from being "sans eyes, sans teeth, sans everything." Adam's prattling may sound foolish to some ears compared with Jacques' polished cadences, but he inspires tender feelings through his faithful attachment to his young master and knowledge of his good qualities; through his simplicity and lack of self-absorption.

Professor Bloom seems taken with Rosalind's statement that "men have died, and worms have eaten them—but not for love," but his love of intellect prevents him from seeing its charm. Rosalind's resistance to Orlando's elaborate professions of love has nothing to do with a love of intellect or scorn for romantic love. No one in the whole history of literature was more in love with love than Rosalind. But this generous love causes her to resist any hint of posturing or selfishness in love-talk. The scornful attitude Rosalind affects toward the rhetorical conventions of love comes from her awareness of human vanity, not from a dismissive attitude toward love. She knows flowery love-talk is often nothing more than a cover for vain desires. The signage of romantic love fades over time and must be replaced with something more substantial if two people are to become "one flesh" and reflect the eternal mystery that makes love so appealing.

The superman also resists love talk—but for a very different reason. Nihilism negates love by negating God and the good. If it is true that the good does not exist and that the cross does not indicate transcendent value, then love is an illusion produced by evolutionary biology and romantic love a sublimation of erotic desires. Rosalind may be skeptical of romantic love, but her attitude is far more complex than the superman's. She does not dismiss it as a delusion. She treasures it and values it while also acknowledging that she is fully conscious of her shortcomings; of her sinfulness, which is the difference between human love and the pure love of the cross.

It is because of this complicated attitude that Rosalind obtains the spirit of enchantment and lightness that cannot be found in the superman. She is in love with sincere love at the very same time that she is condemned by her own double-mindedness. "The good that I would I cannot do, and the evil I do not want to do—that is the very thing I do." But in this deconstruction of the self there is also room for hilarity because Rosalind does not seek justification in herself or mortal powers. Unlike the superman, she does not pretend to be single-minded or capable of justifying her existence. According to her societal given, the sign of love has power to provide justification and happiness even where human agents fail. It is her belief in the kindness of this gracious power that gives her the freedom to be the adorable creature that she is—not Nihilism or the will to power, which casts all the burden of self-justification on the self and leads to the grim results seen in modern literature and art.

Banishment and alienation from the court produce a state of grace in Rosalind and her father and friends. They have lost power as well as all material comforts—and yet it is specifically in this cast-off state that they discover a happiness that eluded them at court. Arden represents the resistance of the soulfulness of the sign of love to the world and its vanity. "Aliena" is what they all are—and yet there is joy in their alienation, just as there is refreshment in the cold winds that tell them no lies. In this sense the conventions of comedy can almost be said to enforce an unsatisfactory conclusion on the play. The happy ending requires them to be restored to their former exalted status—but the cross indicates that happy endings are not for this world. They must be reserved for some other.

Anthropomorphisms

EINSTEIN WAS dismissive of the "anthropomorphic" God of reward and punishment. And yet it seems that he was not unwilling to recreate God in his *own* image—in the image of the genius Scientist who unravels the mysteries of the universe through reason and the force of resistance to divided values found in the mind.

He said some things that are probably a little unsettling to some of his devotees—for instance, that the "religious feeling" of the scientist "takes the form of a rapturous amazement at the harmony of natural law, which reveals an intelligence of such superiority that, compared with it, all the systematic thinking and acting of human beings is an utterly insignificant reflection." Now a "superior intelligence" in evidence in the cosmos is the same thing as a transcendent intelligence. It is transcendent being, not the absence of being suggested by Nietzsche.

Einstein was torn between the desire to seem like a superman—the identity cherished by the prevailing culture—and the desire to assign transcendent significance to his findings. The first desire caused him to refer to himself as an "agnostic," since the identity of superman is based upon absolute resistance to philosophy and its concepts of transcendent being. The superman becomes a superman specifically by declaring that God is dead and seeking transcendent value in his own existence; thus Einstein found it necessary to use the hedge term in order to endear himself to the sensibilities of the Modern age. And yet he also loved the feeling of exaltation he obtained from science—the sense of having a close encounter with transcendent forces. Without this feeling, science "degenerates into uninspired empiricism."

Einstein was not in any sense agnostic if an agnostic is someone who is neutral about the existence of a transcendent being. He wrote that "my feeling is religious insofar as I am imbued with the consciousness of the insufficiency of the human mind to understand more deeply the harmony of the Universe which we try to formulate as 'laws of nature.'" Needless to say, there is no harmony without a harmonizer and no Universe without an upper case. So in what sense, then, was Einstein an agnostic? In the sense that he was dubious about the God of the Catholic church, as he understood it: "Teachers of religion must have the stature to give up the doctrine of a personal God, that is, give up that source of fear and hope which in the past placed such vast power in the hands of priests. In their labors they will have to avail themselves of those forces which are capable of cultivating the Good, the True, and the Beautiful in humanity itself."

Einstein discounted the existence of the "God of rewards and punishments," but he embraced a notion of transcendent being that resembles Plato's Highest Good: a God who is pure intellect and whose thinking is so far above the thoughts of men that to aspire to think the impossible—for instance with the theory of relativity—is to taste the ecstasy of transcendent being. Like the Highest Good, this God is said to be "good" and "beautiful" because of the orderliness of the celestial mathematics that were presumed to underlie the goodness and beauty of the universe.

In other words, Einstein's God was very much like himself. His use of the term "anthropomorphic" to dismiss the personal God of the church may *sound* like Freud—may appear to be a trope of atheism—but in fact it reflects the concept of transcendent being seen in Plato; the notion that God is pure intellect and a force of pure resistance to the unhappiness of existence. Plato conceived of God in this way in order to separate his Highest Good from the pagan gods of Homer, which were clearly anthropomorphic. They not only did not rise above the unhappiness of the mortal realm but were said to cause it through their all-too human behaviors. Plato wanted to give the impression that his philosophy had the power to go beyond unhappiness and provide possession of the good; that Idealism had transcendent potential. This is why he described the Highest Good as pure intellect and a force of absolute resistance to existent values.

But Plato's Highest Good is *also* anthropomorphic in its own way. It does not fall in love like Homer's gods, it does not covet or kill, but Plato described it as pure intellect because he himself was an intellectual being; because he was in love with intellect and its power to make value judgments about what is good. Plato had a strong antipathy to mixed value judgments and the murkiness caused by quantitative methods. This antipathy is evident in his description of the Highest Good as a force of resistance to any value judgment that involves a construct of intellect and sense. Plato's concept of the Highest Good was not anthropomorphic in the obvious sense of Homer's gods, but it did reflect his own likes and dislikes. It was limited in the same way that he himself was limited.

Something quite similar is seen in Einstein and his periodic outbursts of religious sensibility. Like Plato, he too conceived of God as pure intellect—an "intelligence" that transcends the thinking of men. And just as

Plato made the Highest Good in his own image while discounting the anthropomorphic gods of Mt Olympus, so Einstein made the supreme intelligence in the image of a genius scientist who determines the nature of the universe through the forms of value facilitated by theory and its unifying power. The supreme intellect transcends human thinking, but its qualities can be apprehended through reason. Einstein did not negate religion for the sake of science as much as he made science into the true religion: "You will hardly find one among the profounder sort of scientific minds without a peculiar religious feeling of his own. But it is different from the religion of the naïve man. . . . His religious feeling takes the form of a rapturous amazement at the harmony of natural law. . . It is beyond question closely akin to that which has possessed the religious geniuses of all ages."

It goes without saying that Einstein counted himself among the "religious geniuses"—but he unwittingly stumbled into the same trap as Plato and Aristotle by glorifying genius and intellect as the essence of transcendent being. It is impossible to obtain a perfect scientific understanding of the universe through intellect and its purifying power because the qualitative force of resistance found in intellect divides it from sense. Intellect is found in scientists but not in nature for its own sake; thus the attempt to describe nature through intellect leads to a divide in science as well as philosophy between theory and quantitation. The strangeness of relativity intimates a transcendent realm of reality to which the scientist obtains access through mathematics and the unifying power of theory, but this strangeness is derived specifically from the resistance of pure theory to quantitative methods—from the power of the concept of relativity to negate space and time as parameters of physics. Relativity can be used to overthrow Newton, but not without forfeiting the substance that space and time rendered to his calculations. Mainstream physics in the modern era became increasingly detached from reality as it sought a unified theory.

The great divide between theory and quantitation became evident in the ancients. The discovery that it was possible to describe certain abstract figures in rational terms made geometry seem luminous by suggesting that the universe is rational in its essence—that it reflects a Transcendent Intellect which imposes its qualities on existence and can be understood through reason. But the attempt to bring this theory into practice produced divided results because it is impossible to describe nature in rational terms. Geometry appears to have the power to provide knowledge of pure values as long as it restricts itself to lines and simple figures, but as soon as it attempts to go beyond the stiffness of such figures it begins to lose its certainty. This problem was seen in the Herculean attempt to use geometry to analyze the curve of the circle. A curve is more dynamic than a straight line and has more power to reflect what is actually seen in nature; if geometers had been able to describe the circle in rational terms, then they would have gone a long way toward justifying their belief that nature has a rational basis and can be known through intellect. But this is precisely what geometry cannot do. The circle cannot be described mathematically without resorting to an irrational number. With great labor they were able to extend pi a few digits at a time by circumscribing and inscribing polygons on the circle and increasing their sides, but they were unable to overcome the difference between this laborious quantitative method and the sensuous reality of the figure itself.

What is seen in Archimedes is a divergence between the notion that the supreme being is intellect in its essence—and that the universe is therefore essentially rational—and the attempt to demonstrate this rationality through direct measurement. The difference between the unifying power of intellect, which makes it capable of producing theories, and what is actually seen in nature cannot be overcome. Archimedes can *narrow* the difference between the stiffness of the straight lines and the dynamic curvature of the circle, but he cannot make it disappear. His synthetic geometry cannot reflect the dynamism of nature perfectly; and the harder he labors to make this seem possible, the more obvious it becomes that there is a fundamental difference between the purity of the theory and the sensuous objects of science. This is why Plato was forced to abandon physical circles in the end and retreat into the realm of pure theory—but then the rationalism of the theory divides it from the realm of real experience. The unifying theory seems reasonable on its own terms, but it cannot reenter existence without producing divided results.

Newton tried to overcome the difference between theory and measurement by blurring it through the concept of the fluent. The fluent is no longer a fixed point along the curve of a circle, according to him, but a "quantity generated by continual motion." This concept facilitates algebraic analysis of the fluent as it changes direction by means of an infinite series representing its rate of change over time. The addition of time to geometry appears to give Newton far more descriptive power than Archimedes—but it reintroduces the difference between theory and quantitation in a new way. The concept of the change of a curve over time results in two points connected by a straight line, whether it is used to calculate the area under the curve or the difference between an unimpeded fluent and a fluxion resulting from gravity. Newton attempted to eliminate these troublesome lines by gradually reducing the time interval to zero, but then the ratio represented by the fluxion either loses its dynamism and becomes a fixed point or loses its value (is divided by zero). The mixture of algebra with geometry makes Newton's method seem considerably more dynamic than Archimedes'—and yet the net result is the same. Synthetic geometry cannot overcome the resistance indicated by pi to the theory that the universe is essentially rational. Newton's fluxion cannot be quantified as a rational value.

The brilliance of Newton's method gave him enduring precedence in science and the larger culture. His reputation followed an undulating curve rather like Descartes'—he came to dominate science in his own time, went into something of an eclipse in the age to come as a reaction set in against the determinism of his view of nature and the difficulty of the differential calculus, and then rose again when Kant took up his notion of the "vanishing point" and enshrined his universals of Space and Time in the Transcendental Aesthetic. Newton's merging of algebra with synthetic geometry produced more robust results than Descartes' analytical geometry, and the differential calculus was so ingenious that it seemed to provide a window directly into a transcendent realm of reality. Most of all, Newton's quantitative method seemed to have the power to explain gravity and the motions of the planets, which gave it cosmological overtones that went far beyond anything seen in Descartes.

And yet it could not overcome its own limitations. It could not make the difference between theory and quantitation disappear through such concepts as the fluent and the infinite series, and the introduction of these concepts led to results that seemed far removed from the simplicity that makes theory seem appealing in the first place. There was a good deal of resistance to Newton from the philosophers in the Enlightenment, an age strongly influenced by Descartes and the cogito. Berkeley invited his readers to look past Newton's deterministic universe and see nature as a direct reflection of the ideas of God; his attack centered on the so-called "infinitesimals" that are said to characterize the fluxion, but which cannot be finite and infinite at the same time. Hume took up the attack from a non-religious point of view. His argument is simple and devastating—he pointed out that there is a difference between nature for its own sake and the notions about nature seen in natural philosophy. It is impossible to determine the cause that lies behind the effects seen in nature because the cause cannot be seen as itself, and therefore it is impossible to use causal reasoning to draw the type of conclusions seen in Newton about the will of the First Cause. Hume proposed setting aside the complications of natural philosophy and the attempt to read the mind of God into nature and grasping the freedom found in intellect to create a new philosophy based on reason for its own sake.

These were ingenious philosophical critiques of Newton, but they did not offer a scientific alternative to his cosmology. Newton continued to reign supreme in the field of physics until an opportunity to overthrow his cosmology presented itself through experiments with light. Scientists had come to believe that light was a wave, but some medium was required in order for this wave to be propagated through space—the "aether." Using an experiment proposed by Maxwell, Michelson and Morley tried to show that the physics of light are changed by the earth's rapid movement through the aether. Great hopes were pinned on this experiment to confirm that light was a wave and that the aether actually existed, and also to corroborate estimates of the speed of the earth through space; but no effect on light was observed. The physics of light did not appear to be altered by splitting a light beam and running it at cross angles to itself against the onrushing force of the aether (as they imagined it).

Different people drew different conclusions from the failure of the experiment to prove its hypothesis. Some claimed that the sturdy building in which it was performed defeated its purpose by insulating the light beam from the effects of the aether. Others thought that perhaps aether was drawn into the earth's atmosphere by gravity in a compressed way, causing a local steady-state effect in spite of the high speed at which earth was presumed to be traveling. Others theorized that the strange results of the experiment reflected an effect not anticipated by Michelson—that the force of the aether as it rushed against the earth caused some sort of compression effect or distortion of what is seen in experiments with light and thus altered the results.

The explanation that caught the public fancy, however, was Einstein's. According to him, the fact that light did not appear to be affected by the aether wind when set at right angles against itself indicated that the velocity of light always appears to be the same no matter how it is measured—or no matter what the perspective of the observer. The implications of this theory were astounding. Light emerged as an absolute value, while space and time, the universals used by Newton as the parameters of quantitative physics, the very palette of his synthetic geometry, seemed merely relative. Michelson's experiment appeared to make it impossible to explain the physics of light if time and space were fixed values, as Newton assumed— but what if they were considered as one value, as spacetime? And what if this value changed as the perspective of the observer changed?

Einstein's theory might have been considered madness if it had not appeared at just the right time. A full-scale revolt was in progress against the "personal God" of Newton, a devout Christian who thought of science as a means of demonstrating the excellence of God's handiwork. The failure of science to prove the existence of God, coupled with religious wars and such natural disasters as the reappearance of the plague, caused a reaction against Newton's personal God in the Enlightenment and the rise of Deism, with its concept of a clockmaker God far removed from the mechanics of the universe, or even atheism, as seen in Voltaire and Hume. Kant managed to arrest this trend temporarily by taking up Space and Time as the parameters of his Transcendental Aesthetic; but the enthusiasm for Transcendentalism had faded by the time of Einstein. A reaction was simmering, heated by Darwin and his theory of evolution, and Einstein came along at just the right moment to give this resistance the impetus to bubble over through relativity. For if it is true that Space and Time are relative, and not the universals described by Kant, then Transcendentalism is utterly overthrown.

Now it probably does not need to be said that the "personal God" attacked by Einstein was a straw man. It was not the personal God of the text, a God that is love in its essence; it was an uneasy mixture of this God and the God of science and philosophy—the God that is intellect in its essence. There is nothing in the text to suggest that God is intellect, and therefore the text cannot be used to authorize the view that the universe is essentially rational or that it is possible to obtain knowledge of God by using intellect to describe nature in rational terms. Newton may have been a Christian, but his assumption that the excellence of nature reflects a God who is intellect in his essence—a sort of super-physicist—is anthropomorphic, reflecting his own ardent love of physics and quantitation more than anything seen in the text.

Einstein quite literally annihilated Newton's authority as a theologian through relativity. If space and time are relative, then it is impossible to use quantitative methods to reveal the nature of transcendent being. But Einstein also fell short of the "profounder sort" of knowledge he sought because his God was pure intellect and theory—a force of absolute resistance to the limitations of existence, a force that annihilates quantitative methods as if they had nothing of value to say about nature. The theory of relativity depends upon the assumption that light is an absolute value. Perhaps Einstein had an emotional attachment to this notion—perhaps the enduring fascination of science with light raised it unconsciously to transcendent significance in his mind. In any case relativity cannot be tested by quantitative methods because it is impossible to move at the speed of light—to speed the observer up to the point where the effects predicted by Einstein become evident. Sending a clock around the world in a jet is too trivial a gesture to support something as fundamentally counterintuitive as special relativity, and the results of Eddington's experiment are not as definitive as Einstein's supporters made them seem. The same unifying force of resistance that enables relativity to annihilate the Transcendental Aesthetic also annihilates space and time as a frame of reference for physics. But then the "religious feeling" inspired in Einstein by his theory is anthropomorphic. It reflects his love of the unifying power of theory, a love that divides theory from quantitation and restores the ancient chasm between intellect and sense.

Modern science is a paradigm based on the love of theory and its capacity for resistance to the quantitative method that dominated the preceding age, the "scientific synthesis" of Kant and Hegel. The fetching quality of theory is found in its capacity to intimate transcendent value through this force of resistance, but theory founders when confronted with light. To equate the speed of light with absolute value is not the same thing as obtaining substantive knowledge of light, and taking light out of the realm of "thought experiments" and studying it in actual laboratories renders results that point to a limit to the descriptive power of relativity and the insight it can provide into the nature of being. Light has "spooky" qualities, such as an apparent ability to communicate with itself at speeds that are faster than the speed of light, an impossibility from Einstein's point of view. And quantum physics suggests that it is impossible to know the position of light and the speed of light at the same time, casting further doubt on relativity and the notion of using light as the standard of all physical measurements.

Since light seems to resist the ingenuity of science and intellect, let us be radical and consider a possibility that does not seem to have occurred to Einstein. Let us do our own thought experiment and remove light from the anthropomorphic paradigms that come into being when transcendent being is equated with intellect. Einstein was dismissive of the personal God of the priests, but let us imagine for a moment that this personal God is not the intellectual God implied in Newton's belief that quantitation has the power to reveal the mind of God. After all, nowhere in the text is there any indication that God is intellect in his essence. Indeed, it seems that God will not allow any name to be given except "I am," a name that indicates pure subject as well as pure object, pure resistance and also pure being, and is therefore beyond the descriptive powers of intellect, which cannot tolerate a contradiction.

"I am" is not an anthropomorphic signifier and cannot be revealed through rational means. And this resistance appears to be reflected in light—described in the text as a special creation—and its resistance to both quantitation and theory. If light is regarded as an absolute value, then Space and Time are annihilated and any practical application of physics becomes impossible. If light is regarded as a quantum, a practical object of study, then the unifying power of theory is annihilated because the observer cannot be in two places at the same time. Theory and quantitation are revealed to be a matter of personal choice, and the God of science an anthropomorphic God.

A Hedge about Him

I T WOULD seem that the "profounder sort" have foundered on their own profundity. Science was supposed to bring salvation to the world, but just as Newton was unable to unlock the secrets of the universe through his fluxions, which derived their apparent dynamism from the concept that space and time are fixed, so Einstein was unable to overcome the limitations of Newtonian physics by claiming that "spacetime" is relative, since the reduction of physics to the study of light does not render any substantive values.

The Profounder Sort cannot obtain the happiness they long for through their faith in the power of science and reason. As soon as physics attempts to go beyond the mundane realm of "mere empiricism" and obtain transcendent resonance, it is divided between resistance (analytic geometry) and existence (synthetic geometry). Descartes and Kant and Newton and Einstein are divided in exactly the same way as Plato and Aristotle. The scientific revolution failed to overcome the ancient divide between intellect and sense. Any layman who opens Newton's *Principia* or Einstein's *Relativity* is likely to be astonished at math so difficult that it seems evanescent; few are worthy to be initiated into the cult of advanced physics, which is why the equations appear to point to a transcendent realm of understanding. But those who have the patience to search for first principles will find that the foundations on which Newton and Einstein built their superstructures are surprisingly transparent—and their limitations have been known for some time.

There is a difference between theory and quantitation, between pure intellect and constructs of value that attempt to incorporate intellect and sense, and it is impossible to overcome this difference through science, just as it was through philosophy. Newton believed he could go beyond the limitations of the old synthetic geometry, specifically of Archimedes and his method of exhausting the polygon, by introducing the concepts of the fluxion and the infinite series into physics. His differential calculus seems far more dynamic than Descartes' analytic geometry, but in the end it has the same limitation as all synthetic methods—it is incapable of overcoming the difference between existent values and the certainty sought in rational numbers. An "infinitesimal" may draw us somewhat closer to the ideal of pure reason sought in science, but it is impossible to overcome the difference between the purity of rational numbers and the half-steps that those seemingly vanishing infinitesimals represent. This natural limitation of the differential calculus enabled Einstein to supersede Newton's fatiguing incrementalism through relativity and relift theory to precedence in science. Einstein appeared to have found a way to transcend the slough of the infinitesimals by merging space and time and making them relative to the speed of light. But the force of qualitative resistance provided by relativity also divides the theory from the realm of quantitation. Special relativity is a negation of quantitative methods. It is impossible to replicate the conditions imagined by Einstein in order to test relativity, and light now appears to resist the attempt to merge space and time and bend them to the elegance of his equations.

Science cannot reveal the secrets of the universe or provide the transcendent knowledge that the mind demands because it is divided between intellect and sense. The same qualitative force of resistance that enables scientists to form theories about being also divides them from the realm of purely natural things, in which there is no such resistance whatsoever. The fact that it is impossible to obtain a perfect description of nature through intellect and reason indicates that nature is not modeled on rational numbers, which is the assumption underlying the differential calculus as well as relativity; and if the universe is not rational—does not disclose the mind of a transcendent being that is intellect in its essence—then science has no power to provide the happiness promised by Bacon and Descartes and other starry-eyed acolytes of progress. Science can help to bring about material improvements, but it can do nothing to address the needs of the soul, which demands more satisfying fare.

So what was the point of it all—the deification of science that began with Descartes and Newton? The most charitable explanation is that the new science was too new for them to be aware of its limitations. According to Descartes, science has the power to produce value judgments about nature that are glittering, transcendent, clean, true; pure judgments that make it possible to understand transcendent being and find the happiness the old philosophers had failed to provide. His analytical geometry was the first salvo of the Scientific Revolution, a method that rendered gratifying results; but the same love of resistance that motivated him to prefer pure intellect with its idealizing power to synthetic methods also led to a certain stiffness in his results that did not comport well with the dynamism of nature. Newton seemed to have captured this dynamism with his differential calculus, a radical new way of using synthetic geometry. But it is impossible to obtain the pure or transcendent results sought in philosophy by splitting the difference between intellect and sense; nor were lovers of resistance ever really comfortable with Newton, whose method seemed too mechanistic, too complicated, too plodding and dull.

Einstein raised science up to its greatest height in the popular imagination through relativity, a theory that fairly reeked of genius and the possibility of obtaining transcendent valuations, especially since it seemed strange and difficult to understand. The brilliance of the theory made him the icon of the modern "intellectual," with his quirky hair and vaguely supercilious expression; but the same force of resistance that lends transcendent luster to human genius also produces divided results in science, since the difference between intellect and sense cannot be overcome. Einstein's dismissal of common sense as "the collection of prejudices acquired by age eighteen" became a celebrated dictum of a theory-loving age, but a scientific theory that runs against the senses and the information they plainly communicate to the mind is self-limiting. Once the leap has been made that the "beauty" of the mathematics that are used to prop up theoretical science is more important than observed reality itself—than experience—theory becomes unmoored from sense and begins to produce such phantasms as string theory and the multiplying dimensions that are necessary in order to justify its equations.

Modern theoretical science was propped up on the prose of an adoring public that sought redemption in human genius and fervently believed men like Einstein and Darwin were pointing the way to a new Jerusalem. It is now in the process of being undone by a submerged science culture that is wholly immersed in observation and wary of lending its identity to Gnostic theories. A great reversal is underway, now that the paradigms of the modern age have lost their appearance of transcendent power— now that it has become evident that the theories of Einstein and Darwin and Marx and Freud are incapable of making men happy. Relativity and Natural Selection cannot provide transcendent valuations when the same force of resistance that accounts for their unifying power also divides them from sense. The scientist-superman who ascended to fantastic heights in modern culture through the power of theory comes crashing back to earth, like Icarus, having flown too close to the sun.

Meanwhile the "naïve man," as Einstein fashioned him—the man who believes in a "God of reward and punishment"—finds himself in the enviable position of having escaped the collapse of Modernism unscathed. He never bothered to invest his identity in science, and thus his naiveté has insulated him from the crankiness seen in the intellectuals as they lose their status as transcendent beings. Perhaps, then, his faith was not so naïve after all, at least not in the sense Einstein intended. It kept him from counting himself among the Profounder Sort when there was still much that remained veiled to human understanding; when science seemed no closer to answering the most fundamental questions of physics than it was in the age of Newton, such as the actual nature of gravity or light, or even water. In the end, it may be no more "naïve" to believe in a God of rewards and punishments than to pledge one's fealty to such theories as relativity, black holes and alternate universes, which have only the most gossamer connection to observed reality.

The "naïve man's" faith in a God of rewards and punishments formed a hedge around him which protected him from the discomfiture of the natural philosophers. In that sense it may not have been so naïve after all. And yet in another sense Einstein was right. The same hedge that protected the "naïve man" from the foolishness of the intellectuals can also become a barrier to a deeper understanding of being; to knowledge of something that goes beyond the limitations of his own existence. The hedge is naïve because it is a hedge. The God of rewards and punishments promises to put a hedge in place against a predatory world for those who remain faithful. They are told that they will prosper; that their homes will be filled with children; that their enemies will not approach their door. But then this same hedge can also prevent them from going beyond the shallowness of the world and its signs of power. The hedge provides comfort to the believer by conveying status in the world and indicating that he has obtained blessing through the ratio of rewards and punishments—but the honor he receives from the hedge comes between him and the full majesty of God.

The "naïve man" escapes the collapse of scientism unscathed only to find himself confronted with the paradox of Job, the upright man who was blessed with a comfortable life. It was not difficult for Job to believe in a God of rewards and punishments when he seemed to have been rewarded for believing in such a God; but this is little more than a tautology. His comfortable faith prevented him from going beyond the limitations of the hedge that God built around him as a reward for having faith and striving to do good. The same hedge that gave him status in the world also came between him and the opportunity to see the power of God in the way the soul desires—in its immensity. Why would a loving God allow his faithful servant to have his hedge of prosperity ripped away? Perhaps because it is only through suffering and loss that mortals can go beyond the insularity of the hedge and see themselves as they really are. Job's calamity, which seemed singularly foolish, actually singled him out as a highly privileged man. He was given the rare opportunity to hear directly from God.

At the beginning of Job's complaint, we find him sitting in the ashes of his now-ruined naiveté, scraping his sores with shards of broken pottery and advised to curse God and die. He has lost everything, including his health, and thus has become nothing in the world, which measures value by outward appearances of power. But the signs of power seen in the world are not what they appear to be. They are mortal, and to fall in love with the importance they convey is to fall in love with an illusion. The signs of power that provide a hedge in the mind between its yearning for identity and its own mortality are a barrier to knowledge of an immortal power. As long as Job was content to nourish himself on his possessions, investing his identity in the appearance of blessedness they conveyed, he was unable to go beyond their limitations and obtain a profounder understanding of being. Is it possible, then, that he brought his calamity upon himself in some way? That to some degree the accuser is not only the old Enemy but also Job himself, accusing himself of smugness and self-satisfaction? For it is certain that material possessions cannot satisfy immortal longings. The richest man in the world is no happier than the lowest beggar on account of his possessions. The human spirit is too great to be satisfied with material things or the illusion of power that wealth provides.

From the world's point of view, Job seemed cursed, and yet his apparent loss of blessedness gave him an opportunity to see deeply into the nature of being and to drink from streams of living water. Job was strangely blessed—blessed in the unworldly way indicated by the beatitudes. Better to lose the whole world for a chance to hear directly from God than to live in a state of false ease where the mind uses material comforts to deaden its spiritual longings, a gray state of vague discontent and low-grade pain. Job's fall per se was not enough to liberate him from his soft bondage and provide the spiritual food sought by the soul. He had to let go of the hedge in his mind. He had to give up the very thing that is the foundation of human pride and dignity—the ratios used by the mind to hide its mortality from itself—and embrace the nothingness of human intellect and its theories of value compared with the immensity of God.

If God exists, a transcendent being, then there is a possibility of going beyond the gray limits of this mortal life and breaking through to a fresh, new realm of being. This is especially true of the God who "opens his hands and satisfies the desires of every living thing"; who created the heavens and earth in all of their beauty and splendor; who uses such terms as loving-kindness, mercy, patience and compassion to characterize himself; who regards his creatures with the tenderness of an indulgent parent when they are mindful of him. In such a God there is the possibility of something far greater than the placid happiness sought by the philosophers—the possibility of actual delight. But this God cannot be *seen*, and mortals are unwilling to give up the comforts they know for the sake of something unknown, even when they know that those comforts cannot make them happy or satisfy their deepest desires.

Different men have different reasons for clinging to the world. Some, like the rich young man, may see the value of letting go of the world but are held back by the love of money and the power it conveys. Others are detained by sensuality, or an excessive attachment to the ingenuity of man, or romantic love. Job's impediment seems relatively innocent—the love of honor. The hedge of honor that he possessed prevented him from feeling like nothing in the world, but it was impossible for him to hear from God as long as he was clinging to the notion of his own importance. The delight intimated in God requires a clear understanding of the difference between mortals and the realm of transcendent being. Any confusion over this distinction causes them to continually replay the first sin, equating themselves with God and becoming the cause of their own unhappiness.

Job must choose between the hedge that enables him to feel like something in the world and the nothingness that is absolutely necessary to seeing God as he actually is; to obtaining knowledge of the difference between true goodness and the habitual unhappiness of the human condition. This choice is painful because it requires him to die to his own notions of honor and give up something that gives him a good deal of pleasure. He must let go of the flattering identities seen in the world in the hope of superseding their limitations and rooting his identity in an immortal power. The difficulty of this choice is dramatized by the conversation he has with the three friends who come with every intention of consoling him. These men were devout, like Job himself. They did not try to convince him to follow his wife's nihilism, an argument he would have dismissed with ease. No, the pain they caused was far more insidious. They came to articulate, with threefold emphasis, the ratio of being that he himself believed in—the God of rewards and punishments whose blessing can be seen in outward appearances of power.

Job's predicament constituted a threat to this ratio. If it is true that the upright are rewarded and the wicked punished, then Job could not be upright, since it seemed he was being punished in a way few are punished, even very wicked men. Thus his friends found it necessary to accuse him of having violated the ratio in some way in order to protect the ratio in their own minds, heaping hot coals on his head by implying that he must not have been upright. This harsh method of consolation was doubly hurtful to Job. First, the accusation was wrong; after all, Job had been held up by God himself as the model of the upright man. But also the only way he could defend himself was to question the ratio in which he himself believed.

Job was forced to make a bitter choice between his reputation as an upright man and the ratio in which he had invested his identity. The ratio is a concept of God that men use to obtain status as the Profounder Sort—men who are wise and have substance—but it is a product of human intellect and reflects the fact that men are under judgment and cannot obtain knowledge of immortal values through any power they themselves have. God must be something greater than the ratios of value seen in the minds of men if he is indeed a transcendent being and capable of providing the happiness they desire; the happiness indicated to the soul, for example, by the joy it experiences in the overwhelming desirability of a sunlight-drenched fall day. If God is just, and Job is upright, then something must be wrong with the ratio of rewards and punishments by which religious men are inclined to define God and measure their status as mortal beings. The difference between the ratio and God himself is exposed.

The ratio of rewards and punishments is not merely an invention of men. Job's story implies that God does indeed put a protective hedge around believers who are willing to follow his commands. But the ratio indicates the frailty of men, not the honor that Job and his friends were seeking. It is put in place to protect them from their own nothingness, like the covering that was provided in the Garden; it reveals the merciful nature of God, not the power or significance of judgment. The knowledge they obtained of the goodness of God through the ratio was circumscribed by their own limitations. To know the blessings of the hedge is not the same as having intimate knowledge of God because the hedge stands between mortal men and God's immortality. Mortal life cannot be compared with the delight of transcendent being, which is seen as if reflected in a glass darkly. No mortal can look directly upon the holiness of God—the difference between God and men, which is his immortality—and live, because to see God in his glory is to know one's fatal limitations. Men are naïve if they think their ratios of being make them authorities about the nature of God. There is an absolute qualitative difference between intellect and life. They do not know God if they know the ratio of rewards and punishments; they know a hedge that protects them from their frailty.

It is important, however, to stop here and provide a leaping-off point for those who are content with the hedge. The story does not indicate that there is anything wrong with the hedge itself or with simple belief. On the contrary—simple belief is to be commended. It does not go beyond the hedge, but it is wiser than the faux genius of the "profounder sort" who are so infatuated with intellect that they blind themselves to the overwhelming evidence of the hand of God in nature. The wisdom of God is foolishness to men because men are in love with themselves and their dividedness. Simple belief is far wiser than unbelief when "the heavens declare the glory of God," no matter how naïve it may seem to the profounder sort; and Job's story should not be interpreted to mean that one must undergo the trials of Job in order to be blessed or to lead a worthwhile life.

But it does indicate that there is more to God than the hedge provided by the ratio of rewards and punishments. There is nothing wrong with the hedge if it is made by God, but those who long for a deeper experience of transcendent power also will not be disappointed. The superman wanted to destroy the hedge because it seemed empty and sterile, and this resistance was not entirely unjustified. The ratios of transcendent being produced by intellect may seem simpleminded to those who have a thirst for profounder truths—a set of passionless nostrums to be repeated on a three-year cycle with mind-numbing monotony. The "tropes" of the ratio are limited in their appeal. This is not to say they are untrue; but they do not exhaust the possibilities of belief. To know what the mind is capable of knowing about God—the ratios that come into being through the nature of intellect itself—is not to know the whole of God; or, as Job found out, even to know very much.

Job lost his ability to be satisfied or comforted by the ratio when God permitted his hedge to be stripped away. Men come to depend on the hedge, which is why a deeply-felt loss makes them inconsolable. It causes them to see the nothingness of the hedge, at which point they go beyond the reach of reason and the ratios of value that the mind uses to soothe itself and mask its consciousness of its own nothingness. Job's friends did not say anything that was contrary to the ratio as Job knew it; it was not any insufficiency in their reasoning within the context of the ratio that made it impossible for them to console him. In Job's case the ratio itself had been destroyed.

Their arguments reveal the limitations of reason when confronted with loss—not simple loss, but loss of something that has become a prop in the mind; loss of something that the mind has been using to protect itself from the pain of its own mortality; loss of something that enables the mind to cling to the notion of its importance and the meaningfulness of existence. Reason attempts to comfort mourners by restoring this prop and convincing them of the significance of its ratios of value, but reason does not have the power to overcome the feelings of nothingness that attend a deep loss. The ratios it produces are too limited to satisfy a desire for life. Nothingness must encounter something deeper than its capacity for resistance before gladness can be restored in those who have been thrown into the chaos of grief—and intellect cannot provide this something by its own means.

The arguments intellect uses to prop up its ratios of value are limited by the nature of intellect itself. Its quest for knowledge of transcendent being is initiated through resistance to the unhappiness of existence, as Plato said; but resistance is a force of negation, which is why any attempt to obtain knowledge of "being" through intellect leads to value judgments that are divided between action and negation. For his own part, Plato clung to the concept that such knowledge can be obtained through pure negation. According to him, existence is a corrupt combination of the goodness of intellect and worthless matter and must be negated in order to find the happiness of pure intellect. But pure intellect is pure negation and leads to nothingness, the very opposite of "being," which indicates life. Meanwhile those of a more optimistic temperament claimed to be able to obtain knowledge of being through pure action. They believed the goodness intimated in "being" could be known through the goodness of existent values; but pure action cannot provide knowledge of an immortal value when present being is mortal. Our own mortality negates the potential of action to provide us with the happiness we desire.

Any attempt to define transcendent value through intellect and its capacity for judgment leads to the divided paths of action and negation because judgment itself is a negative power. Pure judgment is pure negation, and the only way to overcome its nothingness is to attempt to overthrow it through the pure reciprocal action of intellect and sense. And this same divide can be seen in the arguments of Job's three friends. Two of them tried to convince him that the ratio did indeed reveal the nature of God and that the loss of his hedge indicated some kind of fault in himself. This approach is based on a belief in the power of action to overcome the nothingness of mortal life through the ratio of rewards and punishments. The third friend took a darker view and described Job's downfall as a sign of the depravity of existence. He tried to take the sting out of his friend's catastrophic loss by claiming that all men are wicked and no one is upright, in which case Job's loss simply showed that he was human. But it was impossible for Job to find comfort in this analysis if he was indeed the model of the upright man.

Neither one of these ratios had the power to provide a satisfactory answer to Job's question—"Why do the wicked live, reach old age, and grow mighty in their power?" This ringing question could not be answered by a straightforward interpretation of the ratio because Job was an upright man who had lost his prosperity. Job honored God, cared for the powerless, loved justice, refused to covet his neighbor's wife, showed kindness to the stranger; and yet his hedge had been taken away from him while men who were rapacious and had no thought of God were allowed to prosper. The ratio, then, breaks down in the case of Job. Nor can the third friend answer the question satisfactorily by negating the value of existence if Job was indeed "upright." This friend attempted to invoke the purity of goodness by negating the mixture of good and evil found in mortal life, but pure negation cannot provide a satisfactory answer to Job's question because mortal life is not an absolute value. Mortal life is a mixture of the goodness of life and the evil of mortality, and within this mixture there are degrees of value. Job was not perfect if he found it necessary to "make a pact with mine eyes" in order to avoid coveting his neighbor's wife, but the very fact that he was willing to make such a pact showed that he was "upright" compared with those who have no thought of what is right or good.

So why should he suffer while they prosper? Arguments based on ratios of action or negation cannot answer Job's question about divine justice because intellect does not have the power to provide knowledge of the nature of God. The first two friends attempted to uphold the ratio of rewards and punishments in a positive way, but mortal men cannot overcome their mortality and obtain knowledge of an immortal being through anything they themselves can do. The third friend thought he was defending the goodness of God against the corrosive implications of Job's question by condemning human existence as a thing without value, but his use of the concept of pure negation shows that he was defending the power of intellect itself—the flattering notion that intellect can provide knowledge of being through its capacity for negation. These concepts of transcendent value are not the same thing as God; they are the product of intellect and reflect its inherent limitations. And that is why they cannot satisfy Job.

Job's friends cannot console him because they still have their hedges—it is still possible for them to believe in the significance of their ratios of value and in their power to help other men to see the glory of God. This does not mean they should be condemned for their shallowness. Apparently God permits the hedge to remain in place for many or most believers. If some believe in honoring feast days and others do not, how can they both be right? This is impossible if the ratio reflects the whole of being—but there is something more to God than is seen in intellect and its ratios of value. The graciousness of God transcends human understanding and leaves room for both positive and negative ratios of being. The ratio based on action is right in the sense that human beings have the capacity to do good work. Job may not be able to go beyond the limitations of the hedge through what he does, but this does not mean there is no validity in the ratio of rewards and punishments—in Isaiah 58 or the parable of the sheep and the goats. And yet at the same time the negative ratio that is based on a purifying impulse and would eliminate all feast days is also right, since pure action cannot give Job life. It is true that action cannot fully satisfy the thirst of human beings for life and an immortal identity.

Is it possible that the difference between these concepts of transcendent value has something to do with the psyche of their proponents? That they are optimistic or pessimistic about the possibilities of action for reasons that lie buried deep within race or genetics or even geography? What really is the difference, after all, between Plato and Aristotle? They both believed in the existence of a transcendent being; they both believed that nature was in some way informed by the goodness of this being; they both believed that human existence was a fallen value and could not find the happiness it lacked without returning to a right understanding of what is good. It was not their belief in the good that divided them; there seems to have been something in their psychological makeup that caused Plato to feel extreme resistance to existence and a longing for transcendence and caused Aristotle to feel less alienated from existence and to believe that its goodness had something of value to impart to the philosopher about the nature of God.

As was the case with Job, it was a traumatic experience that led Paul to see God in all of his majesty, as a transcendent being; and this insight led to the conclusion that the graciousness of God leaves room for "each to be fully convinced in his own mind"—that in some sense all three of Job's interlocutors are right because their concepts of transcendent value simply reflect who they are; that the difference between God and men leaves room for many of the apparent contradictions seen in the doctrines of those who believe. Paul was similar to Job in the sense that his hedge had to be ripped away in order for such an epiphany to become possible. The righteousness he thought he obtained through his zeal for persecution was destroyed when he was blinded and became helpless, became a ward of other men and not a ringleader. But through this experience of devastating loss he was able to go beyond the limitations of the ratio and obtain deeper wisdom. God lies beyond the ratios of value produced by intellect, which divide men between action and negation—between the love of feast days and the love of abstinence. It is only when those ratios are destroyed that men become capable of seeing the graciousness of God, which transcends human understanding. Only then does it become possible for them to understand that there is scope within this graciousness for *both* of the ratios reflected in Job's friends. The principle of non-contradiction that animates human thinking does not apply to the things of God; to eternal things. And since all men are divided in their value judgments about what is "good" by the nature of their own being, it is only those who have obtained the humility of this higher wisdom who deserve to be called profound.

Job's story speaks directly to modern man because Nihilism is the annihilation of the hedge—the ratio of good and evil that men use to represent transcendent being. Humankind turned its hopeful eyes to science when it realized that the dividedness between Plato and Aristotle could not be overcome, but it lost faith in the ratio itself when science and natural philosophy also produced divided results. The philosophers began to sound as empty and shallow as the arguments of Job's friends. Modern man was willing to burden himself with the grim ideology of Nihilism because he longed to break through to a new level of existence and forget the foolish failures of the past. That dream now lies in ruins. The superman is mortal, not a transcendent being, and all he managed to accomplish by negating the good was to remind himself of his limitations and increase his bitterness.

And yet the story of Job indicates that it is just at this moment of self-annihilation that we become capable of going beyond the limitations of intellect. Just as modern man exhibits an aversion to discourse and the limitations of philosophy and its ratios of being, so Job found it necessary to get up in the end and walk away from his conversation with his friends in order to obtain the answer he desired. To be in the conversation, in the matrix of discourse itself, is to be trapped by the illusion that it is possible to justify one's existence through intellect. It is to be hindered by the old lie that intellect has the power to make men "like God" through the knowledge of good and evil. This knowledge cannot empower men in the way they desire because to know the dividedness of good and evil is to know the evil of their own mortality. Job cannot obtain an answer to his question as long as he allows himself to be drawn into dialogue with his friends and the vanity of wanting to seem wise about God. In order to maintain such an identity, he must either cling to a ratio that he knows is inadequate or follow his wife's cheerful advice.

There is one more option, however—which is to walk away from human discourse and the futile attempt to justify oneself through reason. The act of walking away from the conversation and standing before the storm indicates an acknowledgement that reason and discourse are incapable of satisfying our deepest desires or providing the identity we seek. It also indicates a willingness to accept the reality of nothingness, since argument cannot shield us from the storm. It is just at this point that Job finally became capable of breaking through the noise in his head, which is the vanity of human discourse, and hearing the voice of God. "Where wast thou when I laid the foundations of the earth? Declare, if thou hast understanding. Who hath laid the measures thereof, if thou knowest? Or who hath stretched the line upon it?" These questions open his eyes to the nothingness of all ratios of value compared with the greatness of God.

The fear of the Lord is the beginning of wisdom. To know the terror of the storm and its indifference to the thinking of men is literally to be restored to one's right mind, a right understanding of one's place in the universe. And then the profounder questions naturally occur.

The Burning Bush

"There is no doctrine more hated by worldlings, no truth of which they have made such a foot-ball, as the great, stupendous, but yet most certain doctrine of the Sovereignty of the infinite Jehovah."
　　　　　　　　　　　　　　　　　　　　　　—Spurgeon

BUT WHO is "Jehovah"? That is the question. To be or not to be is the subject of the ratio, but a burning bush that calls itself "I am" suggests a passionate resistance to the smallness of rational discourse and its value judgments about being.

The burning bush, it seems, is on fire with compassion for its people. It burns with a passionate love for those who love it, and especially for the poor, the meek, the widow and orphan, the oppressed, the marginalized, the forgotten, the stranger, the peacemaker, the pure in heart, and those living in chains of one sort or another. But the fire seen in the ratio is based on the love of judgment—and judgment is a coldhearted power.

There is a fiery resistance in intellect to the unhappiness of existence. According to Plato, it is possible to overcome this resistance by totalizing it and annihilating existence as if it had no value. Plato believed that intellect was "the good." Since intellect is distinguished from sense through its capacity for resistance, he concluded that anything that was not pure resistance was evil. In Plato's view, unhappiness is the result of yoking the goodness of intellect to worthless matter. The result of this unequal marriage is characterized as a vaguely disgusting parody of the good; but he claimed it was possible to go beyond the mixed values found in existence and obtain perfect knowledge of the good by using intellect and its fiery force of resistance to burn up all existent values.

But then Plato's fire burns itself out and results in nothingness. The negation of everything that exists cannot produce any substantive concept of value. All that is left over from annihilating the marriage of form and matter that Plato thought he saw in existence is pure form or resistance—a nonexistent value. Supposedly the *Republic* is based on a love of justice, but justice as it is seen in the Republic has nothing to do with such soulful activities as feeding the poor, healing the sick, liberating those in bondage, protecting the stranger, or demanding fair treatment for workers; actions that are rooted in the value of life. Instead, "justice" is said to be reflected in outward forms of value. The good cannot be known as itself by embodied beings, in Plato's scheme of things, because the good is a force of pure resistance to embodiment. Hence the formal behaviors seen in the Republic are *metaphors* of the good—outward signs of some transcendent value that cannot be known as itself.

Those outward forms are literally nothing in the sense that they have been deliberately shorn of any content. They represent resistance to the limitations of existent values, but pure resistance results in nothingness. Aristotle thought he could overcome this nothingness by describing the good as a construct of value. According to him, present existence is not merely a shadow of the good; the good is actually present in existence as a synthesis of intellectual and material causes. In this view, divine intellect willingly overcomes the difference between itself and matter and manifests itself as Pure Act. Aristotle's concept of the good was solidly rooted in the goodness of existent values—but it is impossible to draw the good into existence without depriving it of its fiery force of resistance. His method of describing value takes the fire out of the burning bush and reduces the philosopher to a cool observer of the goodness of existent values.

Intellect is fiery for two reasons. First, the power that enables it to make value judgments about the good is its capacity for resistance to divided values—and resistance is a fiery power. But Plato and Aristotle also linked their value judgments about the good to identity. They wanted to be known as philosophers, masters of the good; and since they had very different concepts of what is good, the only way to obtain the transcendent identity they desired was to discount any value judgments that came into conflict with their own—was through the sword of judgment. The battle between the philosophers is fiery because it reflects the fear of the grave and a desperate desire to justify one's existence.

This same fiery love of judgment is seen in Spurgeon's dismissal of "worldlings" who do not agree with his doctrine. The institutional church is built on intellect and its ability to describe the nature of God and man; thus the value judgments it produces are divided in much the same way as philosophy. Spurgeon uses the issue of sovereignty to rain fire down on his perceived doctrinal foes. For its own sake, *sovereignty* represents nothing more than the omnipotence of God. But sovereignty cannot be described in the terms furnished by intellect unless it is intellectual in nature—in which case it becomes divided in the same way as Plato and Aristotle, between pure resistance and concepts of value based on a construct of intellect and sense.

It is not the enemies of God or his omnipotence that Spurgeon has in his sights when he fires his withering salvo; it is those who do not share his enthusiasm for the description of God as a force of absolute resistance and pure form. Spurgeon's fiery judgment reflects the divide seen in institutional doctrine between Scholasticism, which was based on Thomas Aquinas and his ingenious melding of Aristotle and Christianity, and "pure doctrine," which resembles Plato and his belief that the good is a force of pure resistance to existent values. Thomas's doctrine tends to take the fire out of the burning bush by claiming that existence can be regenerated by divine grace and contribute to its own salvation. Scholasticism is rooted in the goodness of existent values, which is real, but it is impossible to indicate any kind of equivalence between that goodness and the holiness of God without depriving God of the resistance seen in the burning bush.

Since Scholasticism openly followed Aristotle and his construct of the good as "pure action," it inevitably spawned a resistance movement among those who resembled Plato in the sense that they were in love with absolute values. This movement called itself "pure doctrine" in order to draw a sharp contrast between itself and Thomas's synthetic doctrine. It equated the holiness of God with resistance itself—with the resistance of intellect to the unhappiness of existence—and used this fiery resistance to negate all existent values as well as the constructs of value seen in Scholasticism. If holiness is akin to the force of resistance found in unhappiness, then totalizing that resistance results in the negation of all existent values. Thus the "pure doctrine" produces very much the same nothingness and love of form that were evident in Idealism.

This divide between pure form and constructs of form and matter can be seen in the controversy over sovereignty. Spurgeon's use of the term reflects an enthusiasm for form and its resistance to the mutability of existence. The lovers of pure doctrine attempt to restore fire to the burning bush by claiming that there is absolutely nothing of redeeming value in existence. In this view, the notion that the bush itself—as a sensuous thing—can provide any useful information about what is "good" is utterly consumed. The annihilation of the bush is justified on account of the "total depravity" of existence; but as in Idealism, there is nothing left over from the pure doctrine and its withering fire, no content to fill up the formalism provided by resistance. Intellect sees the bush as a construct of itself (the forms of value that it is said to supply) and matter; when the matter of the bush is consumed, all that is left is pure form—which in fact is nothing without matter.

For this reason, the concept of "sovereignty" seen among lovers of pure doctrine is not dissimilar from the Republic and its totalitarian notions of value. The believer must accept that his existence is totally depraved and welcome the fire of the burning bush—he must allow his existence to be consumed by God's holiness. Supposedly this willing self-negation prepares the vessel to receive the Spirit of God in a new way, producing a total transformation of his being. But there is nothing left of the vessel once it has been consumed. Since all existence has been annihilated as a thing without value, the vessel becomes pure form. It ceases to have any will of its own and becomes an automaton of the will of a fiery God. And this fieriness is plainly on display in Spurgeon.

The word *sovereignty* in Spurgeon's fiery rhetoric does not simply indicate the omnipotence of God. It also indicates a theory of value based on a love of resistance and absolute values. It equates the sovereignty of God with the fiery force of resistance found in intellect to its own unhappiness. Since all such concepts of value are divided between resistance and existence, it leads to vituperation—the only way for Spurgeon to obtain the transcendent identity he desires for the pure doctrine is to condemn those whose concept of value comes into conflict with his own. The lovers of pure doctrine must condemn those who are so naïve as to believe that there can be value in existence as well as in resistance in order to justify their love of pure resistance.

Intellect cannot shed light on a burning bush that is not consumed because intellect cannot tolerate a contradiction. By the light of intellect, either the burning bush must be burned up and cease to have any existence—or it must not really be burning. These are the conclusions reached in synthetic doctrine and pure doctrine. Thomas cannot cling to the notion that intellect is the essence of God and also claim that goodness can be found in existent values without attempting to identify some sort of construct of resistance and existence—and no such construct can come into being without depriving intellect of the fiery resistance it feels in its unhappiness. If intellect is the fire seen in the burning bush, and the bush is not consumed, then the bush must not really be on fire. By the light of intellect, some accommodation must have been made between fire and the bush. Thomas's construct of value deprives the burning bush of its fiery quality in order to fold intellect and its qualitative force of resistance back into existent values. Calvin used the wrath of God and his holiness to annihilate that construct. There can be no doubt that the holiness of God resists mortal values. But by equating this resistance with intellect, Calvin *negates* all existent values. According to his theory of value, the bush really is on fire and in fact must burn to the ground before any good can emerge. The bush must be utterly consumed if the fire in it is intellect because totalizing intellect and its fiery force of resistance results in the annihilation of existent values.

The power in the burning bush denominates itself as "I am"—an undivided value—but intellect divides "I" from "am" through its fiery sword of judgment. If the fire in the bush is intellect, then "I" becomes pure Subject: "I" totalizes the capacity of intellect to resist the unhappiness of its own existence. It is possible to overcome the nothingness of pure Subject by describing the "am" of "I am"—the act of existence—as a combination of intellectual and material causes. In this case the "I" and the "am" appear to mingle to some degree—both are described as "causes"—but then the distinctive force of resistance found in the "I" is lost. If the good is intellect, then it is impossible to bring together "I" and "am" without depriving Subject of the possibility of obtaining something better than that which already exists. "I" can only retain this possibility by maintaining its resistance to existent values. Thus intellect is incapable of comprehending the power seen in the burning bush, incapable of providing knowledge of "I am." Since it cannot tolerate a contradiction to its own rules of reasoning, some power greater than intellect is necessary in order to supply this knowledge.

This problem can be seen in the controversy over sovereignty and free will. How can there be free will if God is sovereign? It is impossible to answer the question by the light of intellect. By the light of intellect, sovereignty comes into conflict with free will, because the qualitative force of resistance found in intellect cannot be totalized without annihilating free will. Plato's love of pure intellect and absolute value leads to the totalitarianism of the Republic. No free will is tolerated because freedom comes into conflict with the purity of his concept of the good. Meanwhile Aristotle's construct of value leaves some room for free will for the simple reason that it is a construct. It has more than one predicate. It equates intellect with the good, but it also claims that the sensuous universe is good—in fact it identifies Supreme Being as "life itself." But in a construct of intellectual and material causes some of the sovereignty of intellect must be forfeited. Intellect must give up some of its totalitarianism in order to tolerate free will, which is why Aristotle favored democracy over the type of government described in the *Republic*.

This same conundrum becomes evident in institutional doctrine. By the light of intellect, sovereignty must either be a totalized value, as seen in the "pure doctrine"—in which case free will is impossible—or it can be said to involve a construct of resistance and existence, in which case free will is preserved at the expense of sovereignty. Thus it is not surprising to find Thomas supporting the concept of free will. His cautious way of quantifying this freedom seems to boil down to the claim that "the sensitive appetite can resist reason by desiring what reason forbids." But then this resistance leads to a loss of the sovereignty that philosophers attributed to reason. If reason is "the good," then either the sensory appetite prevails and deprives the believer of goodness, or reason prevails and negates the sensory appetite. They cannot remain in equilibrium and reflect the force of resistance seen in the burning bush. On the other hand, burning the bush to the ground eliminates free will by negating the predicate of sense for the sake of pure intellect. Like Plato, Calvin openly welcomed the sovereignty of pure intellect and form—but then his theory of value also negates free will. Natural existence is said to be a slave to depravity, and regenerate existence is described in terms that resemble an automaton.

These theories of value have far-reaching consequences. The problem with Thomas's construct of intellectual and material causes is that it deprives the burning bush of its holiness. The idea that the goodness of God can be found in existence as itself leads to such abuses of the human spirit as the "bank of holy merits," where the superfluity of the good works of the saints could be saved up for the benefit of sinners and even sold by the church when a cathedral needed to be built. The sovereignty of God passes in this model into the hands of men. Calvin's theory of value restores that sovereignty resoundingly—but only by canceling free will and turning life into a metaphor of the goodness of God. Adam and Eve did not have the freedom to choose if their choice was willed. The old covenants were shams because God willed beforehand that mortals would fail to honor them. No choice made today by believers has any value because believers do not really choose. Either they are automatons of God—or of the devil.

The problem encountered in philosophy and its theories of value is that the philosophers equated the good with intellect—and yet the sensuous universe is also clearly good, or desirable. In fact it is "very good." The notion that knowledge of the good can be obtained by totalizing intellect and its capacity for resistance leads to the negation of the goodness of existent values, while the attempt to describe the good as a construct of intellect and sense leads to a loss of the goodness of that force of resistance. But there is another power at work in philosophy and its love of "the good" that is not the same thing as intellect and resists the attempt to equate intellect with the good. This power is love itself. This power propounds the confusion of terms seen among philosophers because the goodness of intellect and its force of resistance is different from the goodness of sensuous values—and it is impossible to overcome the difference between these two values.

Plato's way of dealing with this obstreperous power was to devalue it. He wanted his readers to believe that the good is pure intellect, which negates sensuous values as if they were nothing, but he saw that love works against this theory of value by continuing to draw the philosopher to those same values. Idealism leads to nothingness and must be propped up by a tenuous belief in the power of metaphors, while the goodness of the sensuous universe is self-evident and very present to the mind. In order to overcome this difficulty, Plato proposed setting aside love once the philosopher has reached the pinnacle of the steps to wisdom. He claimed that the philosopher supercedes love as soon as he obtains knowledge of the good—"for who desires that which he already has?"

Any reasonably intelligent child can see the hole in this argument, since it is impossible for anything to seem "good" without love, which is the power in desirability. But Plato's anxiety about love leads to an interesting observation. This power resists his desire to glorify himself and his theory of value—but it does not lead to the dividedness seen in philosophy. Intellect and sense are both highly desirable; love does not divide them for its own sake. They become divided by the excessive self-love of the philosophers and their desire to glorify their concepts of value. The philosophers claimed the essence of God was intellect because they themselves were intellectual beings and wanted to glorify their theories of value. But then sense and intellect are hopelessly divided. The burning bush cannot really be a bush and also burning. "I am" is divided between the force of resistance found in the "I" and the act of existence connoted in "am." God cannot be sovereign if there is also free will and the freedom to choose.

But what if the text is right about the nature of God? What if the good is not intellect, as the philosophers claimed—what if God really is love in his essence? In that case, lovers of institutional doctrine cannot obtain the transcendent identity they desire through the fiery sword of judgment. Spurgeon cannot conquer theology through his fealty to the pure doctrine if God is love because both sense and intellect are "good," or highly desirable. The lovers of pure doctrine cannot win the war of theology any more than those who gravitate to constructs of value. Both theories of value are desirable to some degree because both reflect the fact that everything that was created is "very good"—sensuous things as well as intellect.

Nowhere in the text is there any indication that intellect is the good. This notion comes from Greek philosophy. The only value identified in the text with the good is life: "In him was life, and this life was the light of men." Life is the light of mortal men in the sense that it is the one thing they desire most. All of philosophy and institutional theology is a manifestation of the desire for life, for an immortal identity, but it is impossible to obtain this value through the sword of judgment because judgment is a dividing power. The sword of judgment is said to have came into the world through an excessive love of intellect and the belief that the fruit of the tree of the knowledge of good and evil could make men equal to God. The effect of this vanity can be seen in the dividedness of those who equate intellect with the good. But the tree that restores life indicates a different order of power from intellect. "The cross shows us what love truly is." Love has the power to do what intellect cannot do—reconcile men to God and restore life.

Sovereignty and free will are divided by the power of intellect, but not by love. If the burning bush reflects the desirability of life—of "I am"— then there is an explanation for why the bush was not consumed. The fire represents the holiness of life and its resistance to the mortal realm—and yet the bush is also a living thing. The life that is in the bush is nothing other than life; therefore the bush is not burnt up by the holiness of life. The fire in the bush is not the same thing as intellect and its sword of judgment. It does not annihilate existent values because it represents the value of life and compassionate values rooted in the desirability of life—such as mercy, kindness, gentleness, tenderness. It is a fire because these values cannot be found in their purity in human existence. But the fire does not consume existence because mortals know the value of such qualities perfectly well and are capable of exhibiting them in their own lives.

If "God is love," then it is demonstrably true that God is sovereign in existence, since no one does anything except by the dictates of love and desire. And yet at the same time everyone is free in the sense of being able to make choices for evil or good. The lovers of constructs of value believe those constructs represent the good because they find them desirable, just as the lovers of pure doctrine are attracted by its capacity to indicate the possibility of obtaining absolute valuations. "Love itself" does not dictate the choices that are made—but it remains fully sovereign in those choices, since any choice that is rooted in divided desires leads to dividedness.

It is possible to overcome the dividedness evident in Spurgeon's fiery rhetoric and reflect the unity of the spirit of life by giving up the love of judgment for the sake of love itself. This does not mean that lovers of absolute values and lovers of constructs of value must change their stripes. "Let each one be fully convinced in his own mind." But they must give up the vanity of thinking that their theory of value makes them more important than their fellow believers. They must give up the excessive self-love seen in human intellect and its sword of judgment for the sake of love itself, the power seen on the cross.

No Such Thing

SOVEREIGNTY AND free will is really just a proxy war, however. The real battle in institutional doctrine is over "faith" and "works," which is perfectly emblematic of the limitations of the ratio and the divide between pure action and pure negation. The trouble begins with institutional doctrine itself and the attempt to establish its authority through intellect. This authority depends upon the notion that intellect has the power to reveal the nature of transcendent being—which is true only if that being happens to be intellectual in nature. Thus the value judgments seen in institutional doctrine have the same limitations as "the good" of the philosophers.

Thomas Aquinas is forthright about his belief that transcendent being is intellect in its essence. He describes intellect as the "glory" of God as well as men. His belief in the significance of his doctrine is based on the idea that rational creatures can "see" the essence of God through intellect—and intellect cannot see the essence of God unless God is intellect in his essence. But he goes further and declares that "the act of God's intellect is his substance" and that "as His essence itself is His intelligible species, it necessarily follows that His act of understanding must be His essence and His existence."

There are no comparable statements about the essence of God in Calvin. He distanced himself from Scholasticism by giving the impression that the God of the "pure doctrine" so far transcends philosophy and human wisdom that it cannot be described through the type of terminology seen in Thomas. And yet Calvin seems to have shared Thomas's view that God is intellect in his essence. He claimed that God's image is reflected in man's ability to reason. He described man as a combination of soul and body, very much like Plato. "The soul consists of two parts—the intellect and the will." Since intellect directs the will, intellect is the essence of the soul, and, by inference, the essence of God, whose image has been stamped upon the soul.

Nor is it strange that Thomas and Calvin regarded intellect as the essence of God. This notion was almost universal among institutional theologians as well as philosophers. But it comes from Plato and Aristotle, not the text. Thomas openly declared his fealty to Aristotle and leaned heavily on him for his theory of value. Calvin discounted philosophers; but when he felt the need to indicate a preference, the philosopher he cited was Plato. It is possible to have a strong affinity for Plato's theory of value even while rejecting Idealism, the outward manifestation of the theory. Many philosophers and theologians strongly resembled Plato, at least in sensibility and method, even when there was no sign of Idealism in their writing, such as Augustine and Descartes.

Most philosophers and institutional theologians equated God with intellect, but this equation results in concepts of value that are divided by the nature of intellect itself—between pure negation and pure action. Intellect for its own sake is a force of negation. It attracts philosophers because of its capacity to resist the unhappiness of existence, and resistance is a negative power. Plato equated this force of resistance with "the good," an absolute value, but totalizing resistance results in pure negation and the annihilation of all existent values. There is nothing left over from Idealism and its negative power but metaphors of value, as seen in Plato's cosmology and the *Republic*. Aristotle claimed that philosophers could overcome the nothingness caused by Idealism by grounding their concept of the good in the goodness of existent values. But he agreed with Plato that the essence of the good is intellect; and since intellect is a negative power, the only way to overcome the pure negation that results from totalizing its force of resistance is to negate it and turn it into pure action. Hence philosophy has two ways of supporting its claim that intellect is "the good," a transcendent value: either as pure negation or as pure reciprocal action. But then philosophy's concepts of what is good are divided between negation and action by the nature of intellect itself.

This same divide is evident in the controversy over "works" (pure action) and "faith" (pure negation). Thomas tried to overcome the nothingness caused by Platonic doctrine by adapting Aristotle to Christianity. He agreed with Augustine that human nature was fallen and could not obtain goodness or knowledge of God by natural means, but he contended that this corruption is overcome through "grace"—a supernatural power of some kind flowing from God that furnishes goodness to the believer. Grace actually negates the negative effects of the fall, according to this view, and produces the potential for pure redemptive action. Grace makes it possible to produce a salutary description of the nature of God and also to attain to some degree of holiness through good works.

Now for the most part these concepts can be found in the text. Certainly "grace" plays a major role in Paul's writings. Certainly "grace" is said to be the reason (if not the cause) for the new relation to God in which the believer finds himself standing. Certainly the believer who has been saved through grace is said to obtain a new lease on life and an opportunity to know God better by conforming to the holiness of the Spirit. But Thomas put these concepts into the context of the ratio, where they became infected with the dividedness of intellect. Thomas conceived of God as Pure Act and of goodness as pure charitable action. This led to a need to identify some power that can be said to negate the corruption of human existence and produce goodness—"grace."

In Thomas's theory of value, grace negates the negation caused by the fall, facilitating pure action of two kinds: of intellect as it formulates constructs of value regarding the nature of God, and of charitable action, or works of love. Thomas was more immediately concerned with the first type of activity, since his book is the application of his theory of value, a massive construct of the nature of God and man. But many who were influenced by him used his equation of goodness with Pure Act to over-emphasize the significance of good works. And in fact the emphasis on good works became characteristic of the medieval church and its devotion to Aristotle.

But then it also became an unbearable burden to those who were of a somewhat gloomier temperament than Thomas and did not feel capable of redeeming themselves through their actions. They resisted the glorification of works by taking up "faith" and the resistance it appears to obtain to works in the text. After all, the first and most important work is to "believe in the one who was sent." Moreover, those who do believe "are justified by faith, and not by works." Faith can be said to resist works in the sense that it is not the same thing as work—but the Reformers totalized this resistance and negated works as if they had no value. Just as Thomas's theory of value glorified good works by characterizing God as Pure Act, so Calvin's doctrine devalued good works by glorifying faith and its seeming force of resistance as an absolute value.

The reason for this divide is that intellect can only conceive of transcendent value in terms of pure negation or pure action. These are the only two ways it has of obtaining the "pure" value judgments that are necessary to intimate transcendence. Calvin rejected Idealism, but his notion of what constitutes purity was the same as Plato's. He claimed that the goodness of God is a force of absolute resistance to the depravity of human existence—pure negation. Just as Plato claimed that the only way to obtain knowledge of the good was to annihilate all existent values, so Calvin claimed that the goodness of God negates all human work. Embracing this negation is said to facilitate knowledge of God and his goodness. The only thing that has any value in human existence is faith, according to Calvin; works are nothing. The pure doctrine puts "faith" in opposition to "works."

To summarize, Thomas's theory of value, which is openly based on Aristotle, leads to the concept of God as Pure Act and the glorification of good works or action, while the "pure doctrine," which is based on the same belief in pure resistance seen in Plato, results in the characterization of the good as the negation of all existent values, including works, and glorifies faith as the path out of the trap of Scholasticism. "Faith" and "works" are divided in institutional doctrine in the same way as intellect itself. Intellect attempts to assert its authority through a demonstration of the power of judgment—but judgment is a dividing power and produces divided results.

The concepts of pure negation and pure action are like Scylla and Charybdis, drawing the navigators of theology into perilous waters. To listen to their alluring voices is to be enchanted by them when those voices reflect one's own nature and the longing for identity. It is not known why some men are inclined to favor Plato and others Aristotle—but it is a fact of history. Something about their theories of value strikes a deep psychological chord. The Aristotelians are naturally conservative. They cherish existent values and look for theories of value that justify their desire to preserve them. Meanwhile lovers of pure resistance seem to be strongly alienated from existence—or, to put their resistance in a more positive light, they seem to have a predominant longing for transcendent values.

In any case, there can be no question that these two types are real and have been seen throughout the history of philosophy and institutional theology. It is not mere happenstance that Thomas and Kant and Hegel all took up Aristotle's method at such a great distance in time as well as culture from its origin—or that Augustine and Descartes and Hume and Nietzsche all agreed with Plato that the path to transcendence is through pure resistance to existing constructs of value. These two streams of thought are inherent in the human experience. And Nihilism indicates a late-dawning recognition that they are inalterably divided; that intellect does not have the power to obtain a satisfactory value judgment about "the good," which is why Nietzsche claimed the only possibility left for obtaining transcendence was to negate the good and embrace the will to power.

It is quite possible, however, to make the seemingly inalterable dividedness of "faith" and "works" to disappear—by giving up our excessive love of intellect and its capacity to judge value. The philosophers and institutional theologians claimed that God was intellect in his essence, but

"God is love," according to the text—the only essence statement about God that the text provides. This statement casts the question of "faith" and "works" in a different light from institutional doctrine and its value judgments. It removes the dividedness that intellect imposes on value by the very nature of judgment and provides freedom to see the text in a new way that does not lead to divided values.

If God is love, for instance, then "grace" simply indicates the graciousness of God. None of the definitions of grace seen in institutional doctrine are found in the text. Paul uses the word freely but makes no attempt to define it. Any attempt to define grace through the dividing power of intellect leads to a sharp divide. For those who are inclined to think like Thomas, "grace" is a power flowing from God that actually transforms human existence. Thomas needed to be able to point to such a power in order to justify his theory of value—the notion that the corruption of human existence can be negated, leading to pure action. But those who are inclined to follow Augustine see grace in a different light. To them, grace does not negate the depravity of existence. Believers continue to be under the curse of the fall as long as they live in their material bodies—but "grace" provides a covering for their sins. "Grace" gives them a way to believe they have been redeemed even while they continue to feel oppressed by their sinfulness.

These two valuations flow from the very nature of the valuators, and they cause division because of vanity and because of the dividedness of intellect and its concepts of value. Thomas's doctrine does not ring true psychologically. It is a little too optimistic in its view of human potential. Few—if any—of the saints that would be produced by pure charitable action can be found in real existence. Paul provides a profound contradiction of the concept of the redemptive potential of pure action when he says that "I do not understand my own actions. For I do not do the thing I want, but the very thing I hate I do." It is not possible to arrive at a clear understanding of grace through the ratio if "I do not understand my own actions." At the same time, however, the pure doctrine is a little too negative about human existence. The notion that there is nothing good in existence does not ring true. Paul may not be able to do the very thing he wants—but at least he wants that good thing. And in that case he is not "totally depraved." Nor does he say "I *never* do the good thing I want." Indeed, he makes it quite clear in many places that he feels he has done a great deal of good.

The divide between pure action and pure negation seen in institutional doctrine is inevitable as soon as one gives one's attention to the sirens of the ratio. But what if we look at "grace" through the concept of transcendent value indicated by the formulation "God is love"? In the ratio, "grace" must be an actual active power that flows from God to men. The ratio must attribute some causal property to grace in order to account for its redemptive quality. But setting aside the ratio removes grace from the realm of abstraction and mechanisms. If God is love, then the word *grace* indicates the loving nature of God. "You were saved by grace" means that God is loving and willing to grant the salvation that men cannot earn themselves. God is willing to overlook the shortcomings of his creatures in the same way that a parent overlooks the shortcomings of his children. Love is stronger than judgment.

This change in perspective removes the strange disconnect that results from forcing grace into the ratio—the abstract and querulous quality that "grace" obtains in institutional doctrine, when "grace" becomes an argument instead of a quality of love. Thomism results in such definitions of grace as "a supernatural help of God for salutary acts granted in consideration of the merits of Christ." This definition is mechanistic, and its mechanistic quality is necessary in order to support Thomas's theory of value. Similarly, the concept that grace is "God's unmerited favor toward man" is colored with the fierceness of the pure doctrine. The mechanism indicated reflects Calvin's attraction to the theory that the good is a force of pure resistance to existent values. The qualifier "unmerited" adds nothing to the definition without this context. And this resistance is also reflected in the tepid word "favor," which stands in for grace but falls somewhat short of graciousness.

None of the definitions of grace found in institutional doctrine are very gracious. They are based on a desire to justify one's theory of value through the power of judgment, which is not a gracious power. Setting aside the ratio and attributing grace to the love of God produces an entirely different effect, however. Grace does not become mechanistic because love does not function according to the rules of intellect and does not require any kind of value judgment in order to justify itself. Grace is not a "concept," as it is called by those who put their faith in the ratio; it is the kindness of God. The graciousness of grace is restored by giving up the equation of intellect with the essence of God for the sake of the formulation "God is love."

This same gracious effect also carries over to "faith" and "works." If we accept the premise that God is intellect in his essence, then "faith" becomes intellectual in nature. The consequence of inserting "faith" into the ratio is that it becomes a work of the mind and is colored by the negativity of intellect and its force of judgment. But if "God is love," then faith can simply be belief in the existence of God and his kindness. Indeed, this appears to be the type of faith seen in Abraham. There is no evidence of any sort of doctrine in Abraham—and yet he is held up as they very model of faith. What Abraham might have thought about such issues as faith or works or grace is unknown, but we do know that he believed in God and believed that God was kind and cared for him.

If God is love, then there is no contradiction between faith and works, because faith in a loving God does not negate the value of works of love. "It is by faith that you were saved," but "faith without works is dead." Faith is necessary to salvation—no one should expect to be saved by a God he does not believe in—but works also have value if God is love, since faith in a loving God is reflected in works of charity. "For in Christ Jesus neither circumcision nor uncircumcision is of any avail, but faith working through love." Not only are faith and works not divided if God is love; they are inseparable.

But what of the resistance of faith to works that seems apparent in Paul? The significance of this resistance is also made clear through "God is love." Lovers of the pure doctrine seem to feel that Paul wrote his letters to glorify faith and discount the value of works. One can see how they might arrive at this conclusion if they are looking at faith and works through the prism of the ratio. But the resistance seen in "faith" has nothing to do with a devaluation of charitable works if God is love. Removed from the context of the ratio, the clear purpose of Paul's letters is to promote the love of Christ in the church; to encourage the church to fulfill Christ's own charge at the Last Supper and teach it to seek the unity of the Spirit, which is the outward sign of divine love.

From this perspective, the resistance apparent in Paul's use of the word "faith" is resistance to divisions in the church caused by those who continued to cling to the old covenant and were unwilling to accept Gentiles as full members of the fellowship. It is not the value of works that Paul is resisting—he would be the last person to devalue charitable action, which he repeatedly commends and praises—it is the use of the old covenant by Jewish believers to set themselves apart from those who have been "engrafted" into the church through the kindness of God.

In a larger context, however, the resistance of "faith" to "work" seen in Paul is a resistance to vanity of any kind. Anything that makes believers a little too proud of themselves and their concepts of value leads directly to division in the church and makes the church an affront to Christ. This effect is not seen in "works" only but also in "faith" when faith is inserted into the ratio and becomes a work of the mind. The followers of Thomas and Calvin are both quite proud of their doctrines, but these doctrines are not the same thing as "faith" as Paul used the term—simple belief in a loving God. Instead they are works of intellect and judgment. Therefore faith is left over from their value judgments about "faith" and resists their dividedness.

The love of intellect divides the church between Thomists and Calvinists—but not the love of God. According to Paul, "If you confess with your lips that Jesus is Lord and believe in your heart that God raised him from the dead, you will be saved." Thomists and Calvinists both fall easily within this kindly dispensation. "Let us no more pass judgment on one another, but rather decide never to put a stumbling block or hindrance in the way of a brother." Paul is full of statements like this—but they do not play a prominent role in institutional doctrine, which based on judgment. Insisting on pure negation is a stumbling block to someone who is inclined by nature to favor Thomas's theory of value, just as insisting on pure action is a stumbling block to a natural follower of Augustine. This fact is obscured by the ratio but becomes perfectly clear if God is love.

There is room for both temperaments in the body of Christ—as long as they resist the temptation to condemn each other and glorify their own concepts of value. After all, a believer cannot be judged for being sanguine any more than for being phlegmatic. Those who are inclined to boast about their doctrines and rage against the so-called heresies of their fellow believers would have us believe that they alone have the right definition of "faith" and "works." But definition is a work of the mind, and the mind that is in love with its own powers is a slave to vanity.

The Great Negation

M Y DEAR boy, I can understand very well your youthful enthusiasm for the tour de force put on by the good Professor. Wielding the sword of the Great Negation, he rides his dialectical charger to the summit of Modernist theology, scattering his foes like the morning mist of a Prussianism only dimly understood—even in their own minds. Such manliness is rarely encountered; and you, after all, are young, and an idealist to boot. That the good Professor is also willing to boot your Idealism means little in the final analysis. The Idealists and the Nihilists are united in their hatred of synthetic metaphysics and their love of theoretical absolutes. Indeed, Nihilism is nothing but Idealism with all the youthful sweetness knocked out of it.

And certainly the good Professor says many fine things in his book. As I've often told you, the differential method has value in the perennial role it plays as the spoiler of synthetic megalomania. Since no lover of Aristotle was ever more megalomaniacal than Hegel, history virtually decrees that someone like Nietzsche and the good Professor will come along to level the playing field of philosophy. After all, the appeal of their love of absolute values cannot be denied. Who does not crave a simpler answer to life's muddles than Hegel's Byzantine syllogisms? Moreover, who does not like the idea of obtaining a pure judgment that exposes the perfidy of one's foes?

The Great Negation stands in the same relation to Hegel that "total depravity" had to Thomas. Hegel claimed that it was possible to ascend to the thinking of the Absolute Idea by describing a synthesis of one's concepts of being and the mind's resistance to the limitations of those concepts, or their nothingness. This is the same basic description of value seen in Thomas and his synthesis of "faith" and sensuous existence—the concept that pure action can overcome the natural resistance found in the mind to its own unhappiness and enable the believer to "see" God. And just as Calvin used the concept of the total depravity of human existence to discount the possibility of obtaining redemptive value through pure action, so the good Professor latches onto the nothingness of Hegel's own description of Absolute Being to proclaim a Great Negation of philosophy itself.

But the problem with the Great Negation is that it isn't—not really. It does not negate itself and its concept of value. There is a fundamental contradiction in methods rooted in the love of pure resistance that goes all the way back to Socrates. They purport to look upon existence as having absolutely no value compared with the force of resistance found in the transcendent—but somehow their own value judgments are exempt from this negation. You are familiar with the humility and self-effacing humor of Socrates; it's a scam, my boy, a lovely scam. Socrates had to affect humility in order to justify his love of negation, since his claim that there is nothing of value in existence necessarily also includes himself. But there is nothing humble about claiming that one has obtained a perfect understanding of the good. Socrates' value judgments are shot through with condescension that has nothing to do with real humility or a sense of one's unworthiness.

In the same way, there *appears* to be humility in the good Professor's willingness to take up the Great Negation and claim that all of existence is totally depraved; that is, he seems to be willing to negate himself and his concepts of value along with everyone else. But this is not really the case, my dear boy, because he believes that there is great value in the Great Negation. His negation of Hegel's concept of being cannot be "great" and also nothing. The Great Negation involves the same kind of disingenuousness that was seen in Socrates and his claim to know nothing, by which he really meant that he knew the power of Nothingness and its resistance to mixed constructs of being. This power was not really nothing in Socrates' view; in fact he believed that it reflected transcendent value. His love of nothingness, in Socrates' mind, made him a superior being with a superior understanding of the good. Likewise the Great Negation is supposed to have the power to disclose the will of transcendent being and glorify some believers and their wooly doctrines at the expense of others.

The good Professor claims that his attachment to the Great Negation is "existential" in order to distinguish it from the concepts of being seen in philosophy—but in truth it is rooted in the same belief in the differential power of intellect that caused the philosophers to speculate about the essence of being. A truly existential example of clinging to the power of nothingness is seen in Luther. That poor man could not be happy with anything he did, and his nagging self-loathing seemed to validate negation itself as a means of release from the demonic forces that threatened to engulf him. It was impossible for him to embrace the idea that humans can perfect themselves through pure charitable action and other seeming good works—not because he didn't like the concept, but because he did not like himself. The harder he worked the unhappier he became; but he spied an escape from the burden of Scholasticism in the cross, which negates human ambition and opens the floodgates to mercy.

Luther's attraction to negation was purely a coping mechanism born out of desperation—a means, not an end; not a method of thinking about value. He is the least methodical of the great theologians. The heat of his resistance to "works righteousness" spewed into a volcano as he railed against the grosser abuses of the bank of holy merits, and yet for all his spiteful fury he was in some sense a humble man. Or at least his profound sense of his unworthiness never left him and never permitted him to turn his existential need for negation into something as grandiose as a Great Negation. In fact he commented that the lovers of negation had a "different spirit" from his own. He was the quintessential German in his earthiness and love of the good things God had made, including his good Katie and food and beer. The concept that God was a force of absolute resistance to the goodness of such things was foreign to him in more ways than one.

But no such existential humility is seen in the good Professor, for whom the Great Negation is a cold and calculating act of the will. The Great Negation takes Luther's profound sense of his unworthiness, which is confessional, and attempts to institutionalize it as total depravity, a concept of existence; but confession and institution are two different things. Confession is sincere and indicates a desire to lay down some barrier that one finds between oneself and a truly-other that one loves. This makes perfect sense if the truly-other is life itself, by the way, in which case confession reflects an awareness of one's fatal shortcomings. But this is not the value that the good Professor has in mind. His "Wholly Other" is the same thing as the capacity for resistance found in his own mind. Confession, the act of laying down oneself and one's will, is not necessary to obtain such a value. After all, it is not all that difficult to take up the sword of resistance and negate existence as if it had no value.

The Great Negation obtained institutional power because it reflected disillusionment with Romanticism and the pessimism that rushed in as Hegel's construct of being began to unravel. His hopelessly convoluted synthesis did not put people's minds to rest or cause a general outbreak of happiness and contentment. It turned out to be as much of a burden to the human psyche as Scholasticism—actually worse, since the Transcendentalists set aside Aristotle's teleology and took the whole weight of justifying their concept of being on themselves. The synthesis of being and nothingness could not overcome the natural resistance of intellect to its own unhappiness that leads to a nagging suspicion that all of our constructs of being may be nothing. "Being" implies life, and no construct can overcome the difference between this value and mortal existence.

Hegel's failure to overcome the feelings of nothingness that are natural to mortal beings opened up two avenues of resistance. Nietzsche seized on nothingness itself—"nihilism"—to negate any concept of transcendent being. If even the great synthesis of being and nothingness could not overcome our sense of dividedness and make us happy, then perhaps the remedy was to *negate* being and embrace nothingness for its own sake; embrace the idea that there is no Supreme Being and that transcendent value can be found in man himself and his natural capacity for resistance. Nietzsche thought he had discovered such a value in the will to power, which, according to Darwinian evolution, seemed to be responsible for everything that was good in existence.

Nietzsche interpreted the failure of philosophy to overcome the difference between being and nothingness as a sign that transcendent being does not exist. But there is another way of looking at this failure: it can be interpreted as a sign that transcendent being *does* exist and is a force of absolute resistance to the limitations of synthetic method. If Hegel had been able to obtain a satisfactory description of the Absolute Idea, then transcendent being would not be truly transcendent. It would be a merely immanent value that makes itself available to the efforts of men and their towers of rhetoric. Thus the collapse of the "scientific synthesis" can be cast in a hopeful light as a sign that transcendent being truly is transcendent and is something greater than the morass of incomprehensible syllogisms and babbling tower of language put forth in the Transcendental method.

But although the Great Negation takes an opposite tack from Nihilism, it has the same limitations, since it too uses nothingness to annihilate Hegel's synthesis of nothingness and being. Doctrines that are rooted in a love of absolute values are symbiotic—they derive much of their power to intimate transcendent value through resistance to the limitations of existing constructs of value. Calvin's doctrine obtained institutional power by negating the construct of faith and works seen in the Schoolmen, but its effects were not quite as negative as the Great Negation because Scholasticism was built on the assumption that the universe was a created thing and revealed the goodness of God. Symbiotic resistance to such a construct enabled Calvin to soften the impact of "total depravity" by claiming that vestiges of that original goodness could still be found in present existence.

No such leavening effect is seen in the Great Negation, however, which obtains power through symbiosis with a concept of being in which the transcendent has been deliberately set aside. The benevolent creator seen in Scholasticism is nowhere to be found in the "scientific synthesis," which does not speculate about origins and seeks a construct of value in the human mind for its own sake. In fact Hegel's description of the synthesis derives its unique power from the concept of evolution that was gaining popularity in scientific circles at the time. The limitations of the teleological synthesis were well-known, but Hegel claimed that a higher understanding of being had been evolving over the ages through a natural process by which old constructs were negated by an innate force of resistance in the mind to their nothingness—only to give birth to new ones.

The way to supercede this natural evolutionary process, supposedly, was to make it self-conscious by describing a synthesis of those flawed concepts of being and nothingness itself. But nothingness must obtain infinite critical value in order to perfect our concepts of being—in which case it becomes impossible to overcome the difference between it and any finite concept of being. Both Calvinism and the Great Negation obtained institutional power by embracing nothingness as a force of pure resistance to synthetic valuations. But Hegel's description of nothingness as an evolutionary value found in the mind for its own sake is very different from what was seen in the Schoolmen and their equation of resistance with a benevolent creator. Nothingness itself is a purely intellectual value from which any vestige of the dividedness of "the good" has been purged.

Hence, according to the Great Negation, present existence is simply nothing and has no value in it. But my dear boy—is this reasonable? Should we abandon common sense in our enthusiasm for concepts like the Great Negation? You are certainly a humble fellow, and your sense of your unworthiness is commendable, since it indicates that you are capable of seeing the difference between life and mortal life; but are you really totally depraved? Have you never experienced any innocent pleasure? The pleasant dinner with good friends or family; the overwhelming beauty of the sensuous universe which dwarfs the thinking of men; your ingenuity and ability to build beautiful things with your hands; the unseen act of charity and quiet moment of prayer; yea, even your sense of your own unworthiness—is there nothing of value in any of this? Nothing at all?

To embrace nothingness itself is to negate the sensuous universe as if it had no real value in it—no beauty, no goodness. Nature becomes the stinkheap and crackup that we see reflected in Modernism. The situation seems rather hopeless; but lo!—not everything is negated by the Great Negation. That which God made is absolutely negated and of no value, of course, but it seems that real goodness and value can be found in the Great Negation itself. Those who take up this mighty sword of judgment can distinguish themselves as lovers of the good. Or to quote the good Professor: "This labour in the field of the humanities is well worth the vigor of noble and devoted men."

Noble? Whatever became of the Great Negation? Is it possible to cling to the Great Negation and also consider oneself noble? Indeed it is—because men like the good Professor are capable of taking up the Great Negation and using it to annihilate every existent value. The concept of value facilitated by the Great Negation is not very difficult to obtain. It involves nothing more than suggesting that transcendent value can be found in negation itself—in its very negativity, which intimates the negative force attributed to the transcendent being. The humility of Luther, such as it was, is lost, and all that is left over is the smugness of "noble and devoted men" who imagine themselves to be superior to the good things God has made.

But let us keep our wits about us, my dear boy, in spite of the great show of punctuation by which the Noble Man seeks to differentiate his spiritual ardor from our mundane work-a-day lives. Remember when he goes into those ecstatic prosy reveries of his that they have been obtained at a terrible cost. In order to discount our natural love of the things that God has made, he finds it necessary to discount love itself—just like Plato and Calvin. Indeed the poor fellow ties himself up like a pretzel as he attempts to preserve the Great Negation by dancing through a differentiation of eros and agape.

Instance: "Love of men is in itself trivial and temporal" and obtains value only as a "parable of the Wholly Other." What! The love of the cross was "trivial and temporal"? Or is he suggesting that the one who was crucified there was not fully human? The good Professor cannot have it both ways—but these are the foolish alleys that we stumble into when we set out to prove that the finite is incapable of the infinite. Love of men is trivial? "A new command I leave you: love one another." Love of men is temporal? "No one has ever seen God, but if we love one another God lives in us and his love is made complete in us." Was the cross "temporal"? Was it "trivial"? Is this Gnosticism?

Instance: "Suffice it to say that love in this passage does not in the end refer to some general and directly visible neighborly or brotherly love, not even to the love of foreigners or negroes." But why tie ourselves up in such theoretical knots, my boy? Simply for the love of resistance and the power of the Great Negation to make us seem like "noble and devoted men"? That is *precisely* what love means in this passage. In fact the entire letter was written to say that we should love one another and not put the stumbling blocks of doctrine in our brother's way if we want to know the riches of Christ's sacrificial love. Yes, Professor—"even negroes"!

Instance: "In the Epistle to the Romans, to be *kindly affectionate* means—means, that is, when it is understood existentially—to be serviceable, veritable, directed towards the goal, critical." No, no, no, and no. And dear Professor, let us add our own exclamation point to that, and perhaps a thousand more, for even then we would be in arrears. The letter was expressly written to say that we should *not* be critical of others: "Let there be no arguments over disputable doctrines." No doctrinal superstructure is required to give significance to the words "kindly affectionate." Their meaning is plainly evident to any child who does not have a doctorate in "existential" doctrine.

Come now, Professor; let us reason together. It is not difficult to understand these words if we are willing to let go of the notion that the transcendent being is intellect in its essence and can be known through our noble capacity for negation. Being "kindly affectionate" has great value because it builds others up and gives them happiness. It is rooted in the value of *life*, not intellect or its vituperative capacity for judgment. The notion of being kindly affectionate as a "critical" expression of one's existential angst is a purely subject-centered value. The other is left out, his life discounted as if it were nothing. The self-sacrificing love of the cross is thrown over for the cold resistance found in intellect and its capacity to produce proud concepts like the Great Negation. Graciousness is turned into condescension and the death-rattle of library stacks.

And that, my boy, is the real problem with the doctrine of negation, the problem we must always keep in mind when we find ourselves tempted to put too much stock in the thinking of our good professors. The love of absolute resistance seen in his subject-centered method leaves no room for any gracious value. By some quirk of fate the proponents of the method have seized upon "grace" to justify their love of negation—but their expression of this value is strangely lacking in the graciousness and passionate warmth seen on the cross. It is not willing to shed any of its own blood. It is too busy making itself into a scourge of inadequate doctrine and shedding the blood of others.

Saltiness

Edmund Morgan, in his excellent biography of John Winthrop, comes to the conclusion that the "central Puritan dilemma was the problem of doing right in a world that does wrong." From the constructivist point of view, this conclusion is intriguing, and Professor Morgan's thesis results in a profound examination of the impact of Massachusetts Bay on American politics and pluralism. But there is another way to look at the Puritan dilemma. The religion espoused by the Puritans and the empire they desired are naturally at odds with each other. The Puritan dilemma was that the Puritans could not make their religion the basis of a state without robbing it of its soulfulness and its subversive power. And the fortunate solution to the problem was not a natural consequence of Puritanism but paradoxical: they had to allow a firewall to be created between government and religion in order for their dreams of empire to be realized.

Christianity is said to be the salt of the world, but it is salty only to the extent that it resists the rottenness of the world and its empire-producing endeavors. "Blessed are the meek" is not some mere nostrum; it indicates a force of stout resistance to the cruelty of the will to dominate that marks the world and its ambitions. The Puritans did not come to America to be meek. They came to create a bold theocracy. They came to perpetuate the corrupt medieval model that blended church and state; to make it something new and different by substituting their "pure doctrine" for Scholasticism. By putting an ocean between themselves and the king, they hoped to insulate themselves from the Church of England and any interference in how they conducted their affairs, especially from its perfidious prayer book. They came to obtain power in the world—and then they became too much like the world, inflicting the same persecution they had experienced at home on the unfortunate Quakers and Catholics who found themselves in their midst.

Professor Morgan is correct when he says that the shining "city on a hill" envisaged by Winthrop is impossible without good government, and that good government is impossible in a fallen world without engagement in politics. But this constructivist view of the Puritan experiment is a generous retrofitting of Winthrop. The last thing Winthrop had in mind was the creation of a tolerant democratic construct, a pluralistic state with a balance of powers. He thought of his city on a hill as a New Jerusalem. The Puritan experiment was a forgetting of sacred history. Its covenant form of government reflects the covenant of Joshua with his people to join together and carve out Jerusalem, the peace of God, through human strength and righteousness. But this story does not end with Joshua and his successes. The saga of the old covenant shows that men are incapable of establishing Jerusalem by their own means. The kingdom of God is the kingdom of life. This kingdom cannot be found in any worldly power. It is within.

Israel's greatest king provides an object lesson of the shortcomings of human endeavor. He was a man "after God's own heart," chosen out of obscurity by God's prophet, author of the psalms, and—as long as he remained faithful—indomitable warrior against the enemies of God's people. But David was also human, and his story shows that human beings are not by nature the friends of God. Human beings are vain and cannot help confusing themselves with God as soon as they obtain power over other men. David could not be content with his successes, could not resist desiring more. No sooner had he obtained peace for Israel through righteousness than he began to destroy this peace through adultery and murder. His example shows why it is impossible for men to make Jerusalem come through judgment: no one is worthy of wielding this two-edged sword. David's last words are the testament of a man living in profound self-delusion. He did not succeed in establishing the peace of God. His kingdom was a failure—not because he did not love God, but because men are not God, and only God can make Jerusalem come.

David's task, as he saw it, was to create an empire for God—a nation carved out of hostile territory and protected by military power where God's elect could live in safety. But power makes men feel like God; power intoxicates them and clouds their minds, depriving them of a clear view of their limitations. David took Bathsheba because he *could*. He had her husband killed because he *could*. He believed he was blessed because he had power—but he was not meek. Empire gave David the power to do whatever he wanted, and David had desires that were not godly, as do all men. But if even David was not capable of wielding power in a perfectly unselfish and just way, then where is such a king to be found? In the long, tawdry history of Israel, only a few kings remained faithful; only a few evinced a sincere interest in God. If David himself was vulnerable to a fall, then who is worthy to make Jerusalem with his own hands?

The New Jerusalem is different from David's city because it is not a kingdom of the sword. It is a state of mind, not a national state. It is built upon the graciousness of God, not the dividing power of judgment; on the body and blood of its founder, not the blood of men shed in battle. That founder came at just the right time from a psychological perspective because Israel's dreams of empire had been crushed. The once proud nation had been humiliated by four successive empires, the last being by far the greatest. It was difficult for any thoughtful Jew at the time of Octavian and his legions to believe that the empire of David would rise again. The vanity of Israel had been shattered—but for this very reason Israel was ready to receive a new kind of king and a new message. For this very reason Israel was in a position to become the light of the world.

The contrast between the meekness of the manger and the ruthlessness of the empire at Rome could not have been clearer. It seems a new type of kingdom was being established; a kingdom "not of this world"—not made with swords and the might of fallible men but with the power of God. The world is built on self-interest, but this new kingdom is built on the love seen on the cross. The founder of the new Jerusalem did not consider equality with God as something to be grasped—did not seek power in the world, unlike the emperors in Rome who considered themselves to be gods—but allowed himself to be poured out for the sake of the sheep. He deliberately put aside his crown, his right to rule an earthly kingdom, in order to establish a kingdom that cannot be seen in the world—a kingdom of graciousness, the power of which remains hidden from selfish eyes. David was a shepherd who became a king, while the founder of the New Jerusalem was a king who became a shepherd. His saltiness is his meekness and gentleness, which are utterly unlike the cruelty of the world and its ambitions.

Meekness cannot be reconciled to empire, which is obtained through the will to power and the sword. This is why the conversion of Constantine is considered by many to have been the worst thing that could have happened to Christianity. Association with empire polluted the Gospel message and deprived it of its purity and passion. The faith was saltier when it was persecuted by empire than when it became linked to empire and its will to dominate. As Rome collapsed into the "dark ages," the institutional church filled the power vacuum and became a shadow empire—an empire in fact if not in name. The church became like David, drunk with its own importance and full of the perversity and gross abuses seen in the Middle Ages. But the attempt to redress those abuses through the Reformation also reflected a love of empire. The self-appointed reformers did not seek identity in the meekness of the cross. They sought to overthrow the existing empire and replace it with one of their own making.

The radiating effects of this struggle were still visible a hundred years after Wittenberg in the Puritans and their sojourn to Massachusetts Bay. They did not travel to the new world to be as meek as sheep. They came because they thought they had a purer way of making God's kingdom come than their political masters at home. They did not come to put an end to the unnatural marriage of church and state that resulted in the oppressive imposition of the prayer book; they came to impose their own vision of pure worship on all the worshippers in their community. They wanted to make a Puritan "city on a hill," and they theorized that such a City required the purity of a covenant whereby all of the inhabitants of the state willingly contracted themselves to the pursuit of a common goal and faith—the type of covenant seen in Joshua. It was this belief that led to the covenant documents seen in their colonies. These covenants may indeed have planted the seeds of the Constitution—a written political construct ratified by the citizens themselves—but it was not the intention of the Puritans to create a democracy. They thought they could use the covenant concept to create a New Jerusalem.

The dilemma that Professor Morgan identifies is real. He is right to attribute a conscious constructivist outlook to the Puritans and to credit this outlook with their success. The English Puritans were state makers—but this constructivist impulse was somewhat at odds with their enthusiasm for "pure doctrine," which was rooted in resistance to Scholasticism and the Roman church. Scholasticism was a synthetic doctrine, a construct that Aquinas modeled on Aristotle and his concept of the good as "pure act." The Puritans opposed this construct with "pure doctrine" and the notion that God is a force of absolute resistance to the depravity of existence. They used the "pure doctrine" to resist Thomas's constructive doctrine and to justify a break from the English church.

But this enthusiasm for resistance was at odds with their natural constructivism, their desire to make a state. The problem with an eagerness to break away is that it can lead to a contagion of separatism. The Puritans were not like the Separatists at Plymouth. Generally they came from the middle class, often had active roles in government, and did not consider themselves to be outsiders by any means. They saw themselves as purifiers of the existing state, not radical dissenters. They might not have come to New England at all if not for the severity of Archbishop Laud and his eagerness to exclude them from government—certainly would not have come if they had been able to foresee Cromwell. Nor did they come like scattered sheep. They arrived in a flotilla with their royal charter in hand, well-provisioned and a thousand strong. Sensible men like John Winthrop realized that the success of the new colony depended on a willingness to stay together. Roger Williams was reviled in part because he represented a threat to this survival strategy.

It is true, then, that the Puritans came to construct a working, efficient government, and not merely to run away. And it is also true that this objective required them to be somewhat less rigid than the pure doctrine itself. They could not simply attack and expel every Anne Hutchinson and Roger Williams that came their way because they needed all of the people they had on hand in order to make a viable state. But the pluralism that evolved in New England had more to do with generational change than with a conscious constructivist strategy. Just as Joshua's covenant was forgotten after he himself had departed the scene, so the Puritans were not able to transfer their zeal for the pure doctrine to their children and grandchildren. The original covenant was binding only on those who agreed to it; it could not be binding on descendants unless they also agreed. The Half Way covenant came into being because too many of the descendants of the Puritans had inherited their parents' land but not their Puritanism. They were accustomed to participating in town government and insisted on their perceived rights to self-determination. Since there was no difference between the town and the Puritan church, the church found it necessary to make an accommodation with the uncommitted in order to maintain its power.

In other words, Puritan New England was preconditioned for the tolerance to other sects seen in the Constitution by political realism— by the necessity for accommodation and compromise imposed by generational change. Also the covenant concept of the original settlers had long since faded from consciousness by the time of the Revolution. The Great Awakening was mostly a spiritual phenomenon and geographically localized. Very little serious thought was given to attempting to reinstitute the Puritan oligarchy, and few of the most prominent leaders of the Revolution from New England could be termed Puritans or even New Lights. The Puritan experiment died out long before the making of the Constitution and had no direct bearing on its constructivism or system of checks and balances. Most of the credit for the political theory encoded in the Constitution should probably go to Locke, a follower of Aristotle and synthetic concepts of value, and therefore a natural enemy of Puritans and their totalitarian enthusiasms.

But whether or not Puritanism was an active constructive force in the shaping of the Constitution, is now becoming apparent that the Constitution and its prohibition on the establishment of religion has been very good for Puritanism and other forms of Christianity in America. This prohibition reflected the desire to cobble together thirteen colonies that had widely divergent attitudes toward the Christian faith. There were not just the descendents of Puritans in those colonies. Pennsylvania included Quakers and the Dutch Reformed. Virginia was Anglican, Maryland a haven for Catholics. The southern colonies were developing Baptist and Methodist leanings in the time of the Constitution. It was impossible to bring all of these interests together in the incipient empire without stipulating that "Congress shall make no law respecting an establishment of religion."

This prohibition has had a paradoxical effect, however. Establishment of religion is not permitted—and yet America is one of the most religious countries in the world. It seems the prohibition of a marriage of church and state is actually good for Christianity. The Christian faith is subversive to the imperatives of empire. It is built on love and gentleness instead of the will to dominate. And its subversiveness and its saltiness are one and the same thing. The old empire of Constantine and Charlemagne continues to exert a stranglehold on religion in Europe. Christianity loses its saltiness when it becomes indistinguishable from the state; when the power of church and state are linked through institutions that have long since lost their usefulness and meaning; when a rotten spoils system continues to survive in a variety of new forms; when the revenues of church and state are linked; when the state uses the church to prop up its claim to legitimacy.

The unnatural yoking of church and state leads to empty churches and the drift seen in modern Europe. To merge Christianity with empire is to deprive it of its saltiness, in which case it is good for nothing except to be thrown out.

Signs

IT WAS about four hundred years ago that Descartes launched the modern age by claiming that science had the power to provide happiness and prove the existence of God. He believed his scientific rationalism would succeed where Scholasticism had failed by clearing away the fog caused by metaphysics and demonstrating God's existence through the rationality of science for its own sake.

Descartes' attempt to link God to science failed because he believed God was intellect in his essence, a belief that leads to divided value judgments in science as well as philosophy. Intellect intimates transcendent being through its resistance to the unhappiness of existence, but totalizing this resistance as a transcendent value leads to the negation of all existent values—to nothingness. Hence the divide in modern philosophy between nothingness and being. Descartes was a lover of pure values and believed it was possible to obtain such values by clinging to resistance for its own sake—by clinging to the differential power found in the "I" of the cogito and its resistance to mixed descriptions of being. But totalizing the capacity of the "I" for resistance results in a wall between intellect and nature because resistance and existence are two very different things.

Descartes brought back the old dualism in a new way. Plato introduced dualism into philosophy by claiming that "the good" was pure intellect and that nothing could be learned about the good from the signs of value seen in nature, since, in his mind, those signs had lost their goodness through the addition of matter. The way to obtain freedom from the limitations of those signs was to annihilate them and cast our gaze on intellect itself—a theory of value that leads to hostility to observational science by negating all existing values as untrustworthy signs of the nature of the good.

Descartes considered himself a scientist, not an Idealist, which is why he did not realize that his method would have the same effect as Idealism. Unlike Plato, he did not discount the value of the sensuous universe or observational science; his concept was that it was possible to use pure intellect to purify science. But Descartes did not foresee that his love of pure intellect would devalue the signs found in nature and deprive them of their transcendent significance. If the good really is intellect, as the philosophers claimed, then the goodness seen in nature can obtain transcendent significance in only two ways. Either it can be said to point to a transcendent intellect that is a force of pure resistance—a description that devalues nature by drawing a line between sensuous things and "the good." Or it can be described as a construct of intellect and matter; for instance as a synthesis of intellectual and material causes, in which case it appears to be a solid and reliable sign of the nature of transcendent being.

One such construct was Scholasticism. Descartes resisted the complications of this construct by claiming that pure intellect had the power to cut through the muddles caused by its metaphysics and clarify transcendent being. He thought the cogito would enable scientists to read the mind of God directly in nature and its signs of value; but in fact it led to the devaluation of those signs by emphasizing the goodness of intellect over existent values. The only thing that has existent value in the cogito is thinking itself. The cogito glorifies the capacity of intellect to doubt Scholasticism, but Descartes' celebration of this capacity for doubt led to the opposite of what he desired—to radical skepticism in Hume, both about the power of science to reveal anything of value about transcendent being, and even of the existence of transcendent being itself.

The wall between pure intellect and observational science can be seen in Descartes' analytical geometry, which he used to represent his ideal of rational perfection. The very purity of the system leads to abstraction and divides it from nature itself. It cannot amount to anything more than a metaphor of the value of nature, a story told on two planes that never intersect and must be interpreted, since it is possible to use Descartes' geometry without thinking of nature at all. The capacity of intellect to produce rational values through its force of resistance leads to a negation of the dynamic values of existence, which are not rational in nature. Newton's synthetic geometry is specifically a reaction to this limitation. The results produced by analytical geometry were too remote from nature to have scientific value or provide much substantive information about the nature of the good, so Newton set out to correct this deficiency by describing a construct of nature and the purity found in intellect and its force of resistance.

Like Descartes, Newton thought of science as a means of obtaining insight into the mind of God. He attempted to supply the dynamism that was missing in Descartes' geometry by splitting the difference between the reality of nature and the ideality of intellect and its qualitative force of resistance. But this is impossible without sacrificing ideality for the sake of dynamism—without sacrificing the purity and simplicity that Descartes sought in scientific rationalism. Newton claimed it was possible to describe a vanishing point between nature and intellect through his differential method, but this vanishing point can never actually vanish. It can never become *pure* or obtain the transcendent resonance that both Descartes and Newton attributed to intellect.

The age of science began with great excitement over the apparent power of natural philosophy to go beyond the limitations of Idealism and Realism and provide happiness by interpreting the signs of transcendent being in nature. But it led to the same dividedness as Greek philosophy by equating God with intellect and its qualitative force of resistance. Descartes' method devalued the signs found in nature by emphasizing the goodness of resistance, while Newton's method made those signs seem oppressively complex by attempting to link them to his calculus of middle terms between intellect and sense.

This dividedness led to a new enthusiasm in science—for "naturalism," or resistance to the very notion that the goodness of nature is a sign of transcendent being. The naturalists attempted to obtain knowledge of transcendent value in exactly the opposite way from Descartes and Newton—by annihilating any thought of transcendent being or the value of signs; by declaring the death of God and seeking happiness in existence for its own sake; by attempting to substitute the totalizing power of theory for transcendent being. If it can be demonstrated that the values found in nature came into being without the help of a transcendent power, then it becomes possible to negate the old philosophy and its concept that nature is a mixture of intellect and matter. It becomes possible to go beyond the dividedness seen in Newton and Descartes and their theories of value.

Darwin's theory produced great excitement by purporting to show that nature was capable of producing such great values as life and beauty of its own accord. He attributed this amazing ameliorative capacity to the supposed totalizing power of the survival of the fittest. Then Einstein made a mighty contribution to naturalism by indicating that the God of Kant and the Transcendentalists was an illusion. They based their construct of being on the supposed irreducibility of Time and Space and the limits they imposed on science. But Einstein's theory made it seem that Time and Space were merely relative, thus smashing Newton's clockmaker God to pieces.

Darwinism and relativity are both based on the notion that the signs of value seen in nature are not what they appear to be. According to Darwin, the beauty of the species is not a sign of a transcendent intellect imposing its forms of value on existence, as the philosophers supposed; instead it is the result of a mysterious discretionary power found in nature itself called "natural selection." Similarly the constructs of transcendent being seen in Newton and the Transcendentalists are not sound, Einstein's theory implies, because the signs of value they thought they saw in nature are not what they appear to be. Relativity leads to the conclusion that those signs are an illusion, very much like Idealism. The age of science began with the attempt to find happiness by interpreting the transcendent significance of the signs of value seen in nature, and when that effort failed it attempted to go beyond the limitations of "natural philosophy" through naturalism—by negating God and claiming those signs have no such significance at all.

But there is another way to look at nature and its signs of value—a way that does not lead to the fatal divide seen between Newton and Descartes. They were divided between intellect and sense because they were in love with intellect and its sword of judgment. They believed they could use this sword to obtain precedence in the world of philosophy, which is why they equated intellect with the essence of God. Philosophy led to divided descriptions of the signs of nature because of the vanity of its practitioners. Descartes literally equated life with his ability to think; indeed, the cogito seems to give intellect precedence to life. But the first distinction between Descartes and transcendent being is that Descartes is mortal. It is presumptuous for mortals to believe they can raise themselves up to knowledge of immortal value through a method of thinking.

It is possible to go beyond the limitations of "natural philosophy," however, and its interpretations of the signs of value found in nature. Just because the theories of value propounded by Descartes and Newton led to divided descriptions of those signs does not mean that they have no transcendent significance. This dividedness indicates the limitations of natural philosophy but not of the signs themselves. In fact those signs are now in the process of exposing the limitations of naturalism and the attempt to obtain scientific knowledge through Nihilism. In order to justify their theory of value, the naturalists must demonstrate that the goodness evident in nature is the result of purely natural processes and does not indicate the influence of a transcendent being—but the more we know about that goodness, the less likely this seems.

The philosophers were in love with intellect and its theories of value, but the major ingredient in value is *desirability*. By this measure it is becoming increasingly clear that nature is "very good." The beauty of nature, for example, is overwhelmingly evident. This beauty intimates transcendent being in two ways: first, through its great desirability; and also because of the difficulty human beings encounter when they attempt to create something beautiful themselves. This difficulty indicates that beauty cannot come into existence easily or be accounted for by theories of value that are rooted in a love of pure intellect and its capacity to produce simple valuations, such as the survival of the fittest. Plato muddled the issue by claiming that God is intellect and that natural beauty reflects the differential power found in intellect, a theory that leads to dualism and the negation of existent beauty. But no such dividedness is seen in beauty from the point of view of desirability. The beauty of nature is overwhelmingly desirable, and naturalists cannot account for this desirability through purely natural means. It must be attributed either to some discretionary power in nature itself, such as "natural selection"—which then becomes tantamount to God—or to pure chance, which seems unlikely.

Moreover, it is now becoming evident that beauty is only one possible sign of transcendent being in nature. Science has been in the process of discovering an unseen realm of reality that is "good" in the sense of being astonishingly functional. In this hidden realm, the most forceful sign of transcendent being is the value of life. Darwin made life out to be a relatively simple value in order to suit his love of the unifying power of theory; but the more we know about life, the more implausible his theory begins to seem. It turns out that life is so complex that it begins to seem almost evanescent. It is based on a code of such intricacy that the odds against it having come into being by chance are implausibly high. This same complexity is seen in the living cell, a self-contained system made up of interrelated and indispensable parts. Hearing and vision are highly complex processes and cannot be described by simple means. There are *complementary* systems that support life, such as the sympathetic and parasympathetic nervous systems. Complementary systems are naturally complex—are a construct—but the complexity of those systems transcends science when it is encountered in such substances as cAMP and cGMP or in the cyclooxygenase cascade, which are so complex as to seem circular.

The complexity of these systems defies the limitations of theory and the love of simplicity that it reflects. The chance of DNA assembling itself in a useful form of its own accord is infinitesimally small. This is not a question of belief or unbelief but pure statistics. And this seeming impossibility is multiplied many times over at each level of functionality necessary to support life. The question basic science is raising today is not whether Descartes' God or Newton's God is preferable to the naturalism of Darwin; the question is whether naturalism has the descriptive power to account for the marvelous complexity of life. This question also applies at the cosmological level, since the earth now appears to be an environment designed to support life. Again, it is not a matter of whether Newton or Einstein had the better explanation for the orbit of the planets or the effects of gravity. The question is far more basic. Would life even be possible if the earth were not in almost its precise orbit; if its tilt or rate of rotation were slightly different; if the energy emanating from the sun did not remain constant over long periods of time; if the elements were not constant and did not demonstrate affinity. A great deal of fine tuning appears to have gone into the possibility of life on earth. Can naturalism account for it? And if not, when does this fine tuning become a sign of transcendent being?

Everyone knows about the limitations of Descartes and Kant and their attempts at ascribing transcendent significance to nature and its signs of value. Those attempts led to highly divided valuations because Descartes and Kant were in love with intellect and its dividing power. But the new discoveries in science, which are not ideological in nature, seem to be illuminating the goodness of a value that is not the same thing as intellect and does not exhibit its dividedness—the value of life. It is not intellect, the god of philosophy, that is glorified in the new science; it is life. And contrary to what is implied in the cogito, these are two very different values. New discoveries in science indicate the *goodness* of life. Our growing awareness of this goodness enables us to fill the vacuum caused by the collapse of natural philosophy and its theories of transcendent being.

As the most desirable value known to man, life becomes the "light of men" and a new way of looking at value. This change has profound implications. First, it validates Nihilism, or at least the annihilation of philosophy. The goodness evident in life leaves no room for the desire to restore the empires of the past. The transcendent being of the philosophers truly is "dead," annihilated by the natural force of resistance found in intellect to its dividedness. It is not possible to go beyond Nihilism by attempting to resurrect "being" through some new theory of value; Nihilism indicates a collective awareness of the limitations of all such theories. But the goodness of life makes it possible to go beyond Nihilism because life is not the same thing as intellect. Nihilism negated the value of "being" as described by the philosophers—but "being" is not life. The dividedness of "being" reflects the deification of intellect seen in philosophy, since intellect is a dividing power; but life does not depend upon intellect and is not a divided value.

What knowledge can be derived from the emergence of life as a transcendent value? Much in every way. The desirability of life illuminates both a means of obtaining knowledge of value and also a way of being that does not lead to the dividedness seen in philosophy. Life casts light on the question of how to be. The commandments, the admonitions in the Sermon on the Mount, the letters of Paul—all of these obtain a new significance through the value of life. Viewing them from this perspective is like turning on a light and discovering that they are something more than rote instructions or empty rules. They are not merely doctrine. Their content is the value of life, and their purpose is to point the way to a happy and satisfying existence.

To extend this tangible benefit, the resistance of life and its goodness to the limitations of our concepts of "being" also provides a way to look past the limitations of the institutional church. All institutional doctrine is built on intellect and its power to provide a description of the nature of God and man; this is why all doctrine is naturally divided in the same way as Plato and Aristotle, between pure values and ratios of value. It becomes possible to look past those limitations, however, through the value of life; both to understand why they are limited, and to seek a desirable identity in the resistance provided by the goodness of life to the smallness of the institution and its concepts of value.

Nature is certainly "good," or highly desirable, but the signs of value seen in nature cannot obtain transcendent significance through the theories of value seen in philosophy, which are rooted in the love of intellect. They obtain this significance through the value of life, a value that illuminates a new way to go beyond the limitations of natural philosophy as well as of naturalism and its futile resistance to "the good."

Letter to a Friend

MY DEAR friend, what you say is very true. You remembered the gracious work in which there was no toil, since someone else had done it. There was bread to eat and wine to drink in this work, without money and without cost; and they were imperishable.

Dazzled by the reappearance of the argument, you clung to it with all of your might—the argument that divides faith from works in order to condemn division and recommend the reconciling power of love. But by clinging to the argument, you missed the meaning and became yourselves a force of division.

You became strong in argument and gained power in the world, but if you had understood the meaning you would have hated the world and longed to be weak—because the strength of God is made known in our weakness.

God gives life, but judgment brings death.

The argument divides faith from works in order to condemn the arguing and judgment that were seen in the early church between gentile and Jew. Men seek to raise themselves up and become strong through their arguments—but to be strong in the world is to be weak in the graciousness of God.

The argument exposes the shortcomings of those who seek to boast of their works, of being stewards of the law, since "all have fallen short of the glory of God." They had no reason to boast of obedience when they too were sensual, proud and cruel.

The law is based on love, and therefore the law cannot be used to judge others. It cannot be used to glorify some mortals, who are under judgment on account of their mortality, at the expense of others.

The law is summed up in the command to do no harm to one's neighbor—but they made the law unkind by using it to boast about themselves. They became experts in the letter of the law, its force of division, but in their love of judgment they mocked the generous spirit of the law, which preserves life.

Those who had the law belied the spirituality of the law by boasting about the works of mortal flesh.

As God has been merciful to us, let us be merciful to one other.

The argument divides faith from works in order to condemn those who boast of their works—but the meaning, my dear friend, is just the opposite of division. It is the good work of reconciliation.

The hardest work is to be reconciled to those who are different from ourselves; to let go of our false pride for the sake of a higher calling. Therefore the argument does not condemn work—it recommends it by condemning our desire to boast about our works.

Kindness is work, and it is not merely shown in the active work of charity; it is also seen in the willingness to be completely humble and gentle and lay down the sword of judgment, the first and indispensable step toward reconciliation.

Laying down this sword is a great and good work, my dear friend, and it is this work that the argument recommends—not judgment; not argument itself.

It is the kindness of God that leads to repentance.

We ourselves teach that God came in mercy, not judgment, not with a sword but in a stable; not in strength but perfect meekness. Why then do we continue cling to the argument and its sword of judgment, and not to the meaning, which is love?

Do we believe that it is possible to find what we are looking for through judgment and its dividing power? Are we willing to be judged? Have we become so proud of ourselves and our doctrine that we have no healthy fear of God and his holiness?

It was not by judgment that we were reconciled to God but by love; not by the righteousness of doing or thinking but by the cross, which shows us what love truly is. If we who have been reconciled by kindness do not show kindness to others—if we judge them—then we are like the ungrateful servant to whom much has been forgiven.

The one whom we claim as our savior opened up his hands for the place where the nails went in. Why then do we continue to cling to the argument? Must we not also open us our hands if we wish to emulate him? Can the servant be greater than his master?

Stop judging by appearances.

Men are mortal and fear nothingness. This is why they use the power of judgment to compare themselves with others, hoping to overcome nothingness by raising themselves up at the expense of their fellow beings.

But judgment is rooted in law, and the significance of the law is hidden from the eyes of grasping men. The law is summed up in the command to love one another. Since judgment brings pain to others, it is impossible to cling to judgment and also be obedient to the law.

Do some men have different doctrines from us? Do they appear strange to our eyes? No one can judge by appearances because the law is the argument and not the meaning. The sword of law is a dividing power, but the meaning of the law is love.

"Circumcision is indeed of value if you obey the law"—when it signifies consecrating oneself to the Spirit of life. Circumcision is the outward sign, but the meaning is to circumcise our hearts of human pride. Thus those who use the outward sign to glorify themselves are making a mockery of the law.

Fasting is of value when it indicates that we are natural enemies of God, creatures of appetite, and need to take drastic measures to remind ourselves of what is good. But if we are God's enemies, then what good is fasting when we use it to glorify ourselves?

Men use outward signs to make themselves seem holy—but God looks upon the heart. It is not circumcision or fasting that makes men holy; it is an attitude of repentance through which they obtain access to the throne of grace.

You who boast about the law, do you dishonor God
by breaking the law?

The law says, Do not murder. But can I make myself holy by refraining from murder? If I have I refrained from murdering, then I must have desired to murder. Therefore I have broken the law.

The law is powerful, but law cannot make men holy because law obtains power through the unholiness of men. The law has power only because men are unholy. Therefore no one can use the law to justify himself at the expense of others.

To judge others is to break the law because the law is summed up in the command to love one another. Those who boast of their obedience to the law dishonor God and his holiness.

It is by faith that you have been saved, not by works,
lest any man should boast.

The sword of the argument divides faith from works—but not to condemn works. Faith and works are divided to condemn boasting—whether about works or "faith."

The argument uses the sword of judgment to divide, but the sign of life is unity. The church must be reconciled and live a life of love in order for the Spirit to be glorified and be seen in its fellowship in all its glory.

This is the meaning—but we continue to cling to the argument and its dividing power. Why condemn work as if it were nothing? It is not work that is condemned by the argument, but boasting. Indeed, reconciliation is a work of love.

Doctrines are obtained by using the mind and its dividing power to make judgments about faith. They are not faith; they are works of the mind. But if our doctrines are works, then the sword of the argument prevents us from boasting about them.

There are many types of boasting—not just about works of the law. Boasting was seen in the Jews who thought they could justify themselves by work as well as in the gentiles who thought that their faith provided freedom from the law.

Boasting is also seen in those who believe that their doctrines, their works of the mind, make them superior to believers whose minds work in other ways. What we think is work; but if what we think leads to division and not the unity of the Spirit of life, then we have nothing to boast about.

All boasting is an enemy to reconciliation and the Spirit of life. Therefore all forms of boasting are condemned.

If I must boast, I will boast of the things
that show my weakness.

Come, let us reason together. Is it the purpose of our doctrines to show our weakness? On the contrary—is not the purpose of doctrine to demonstrate the strength of our arguments?

If our arguments have power, then how do they show weakness? If we boast of our doctrines by using them to condemn others, are we boasting in the things that show our weakness? Or are we boasting about the strength of our doctrines?

We are boasting when we cling to the argument that divides faith from works because we believe that this argument makes us strong. But in fact the argument makes us weak and indefensible by destroying the unity of the believers.

If the meaning is reconciliation, then why boast about the argument? Do we think we can justify ourselves through its sword of judgment? If this sword divides us, then it cannot be justified. We are condemned by the Spirit of life.

> *Since the righteousness that comes by faith is a gift,*
> *let us enjoy the gift in peace.*

Now the meaning finally appears—are we too infatuated with the argument to see it? The argument uses the sword of judgment to chasten and make us think soberly about ourselves. But the meaning cannot be found in the sword, a dividing power. The meaning is reconciliation.

The argument uses the sword of judgment to separate faith from works in order to show that works cannot be used to justify us or make us seem more important than others; to condemn any boasting about works. We have no right to boast about our works, since justification comes by faith, and faith is a gift and not a work.

This argument opens the door for reconciliation because all are equal in the gift of faith. If some believers think they are better than others, then there can be no unity in the church. Their boasting destroys unity. But there is no room for boasting if we are justified by faith and faith is a gift.

The apostle uses the gift of faith to vanquish boasting. But faith is not the same thing as the argument. Faith is a gift and cannot be obtained by mortal means. It is by faith that men avoid the sword of judgment—but then faith cannot be made into a sword for condemning others.

If justification comes by faith, and faith is a gift, then men have no reason to boast about what they believe. Boasting violates the gracious spirit of the gift.

> *Let no debt remain outstanding except*
> *the debt to love one another.*

We owe a debt on account of the love that was shown on the cross, a debt to love one another. Only by this love does it become evident whom we follow—not by the arguments of any doctrine.

The Spirit of life cannot be seen in the church unless the faithful give up boasting of all kinds—whether over works or over doctrine. The only way to reflect the Spirit of life is to be completely humble and gentle, since all men are mortal. Boasting does not reflect life; it reflects our own mortality.

The letter implores us in heartfelt terms to cling to the graciousness of the cross in our relations with our fellow believers. "Enjoy the gift in peace"—that is the meaning. The dividing power of the argument is no longer present in the meaning because there can be no peace in argument.

The argument—the sword of judgment—consumes itself and disappears, just as death has been swallowed up in life.

The gift is a gift because it is not a work.

Faith is a gift. Let us cling to the sweetness of the gift and give up the bitter arguments through which we seek to justify our doctrines. No one has the right to boast about something he did not earn; therefore boasting is excluded by the graciousness of the gift.

The "light of the world" showed us what true righteousness is by laying down his life so that we could be reconciled to God. In the same way, it is only by laying down our own lives and the power of judgment that we can be reconciled to others.

He sacrificed himself so that we could eat the bread of righteousness and be blessed with the spirit of life, which is seen in reconciliation and in peace. But this living bread can have no effect if we continue to feed on the yeast of argument, which puffs men up and causes them to think highly of themselves.

The path to life is through the gift of faith and the gentleness and kindness of the cross. Do not be deceived. Nothing else can save us.

To one who works, his wages are not reckoned
as a gift but as his due.

"Aha!" we say—still clinging to the argument and not the meaning—"this means that work is of no importance."

But—"Was not our father Abraham justified by works, when he had offered Isaac his son on the altar?" And are we not told that our day will break forth and we will be healed if we observe true fasting—if we feed the hungry and clothe the poor, if we break every yoke and set those who are in bondage free?

Or is the word that we received a lie?

To him who does not work, but trusts in him who justifies the ungodly,
his faith is reckoned as righteousness.

"Aha!" we say—still clinging to the dividing power of the argument and not the meaning— "this means that works have no value."

But what about the good work of believing in Him? What about the sheep and the goats? What about reconciliation and living in peace?

The apostle seeks to encourage reconciliation by reminding us that believing is the first and most important "good work." If we are justified by this faith, then we cannot use our works to glorify ourselves at the expense of others.

He uses the sword of judgment to condemn the divisions that result from reveling in our works and using them to distinguish ourselves as holy men. But the meaning of the argument is reconciliation, which is higher than judgment.

Spiritual Discernment

My dear friend, can we be so blind? The meaning is that we should stop judging one another and live in peace—but then the meaning cannot be the same thing as the argument, which is rooted in judgment and its dividing power.

What are the "sufferings" in which we are counseled to rejoice? The sufferings we bring on ourselves through our futile arguments over "faith" and "works"? Or the sufferings of the cross, where all judgment was laid aside for the sake of love?

Love entails suffering, since we must put our selfish desires on the cross. But just as God reconciled himself to us by laying down his life, so we can be reconciled to others when we lay down our lives and seek to imitate his graciousness and mercy.

Ye are not under law, but under grace.

The cross was gracious, and graciousness is the mark of those who take up his cross and follow him. But judgment is not gracious. Judgment is a sword. Those who turn to judgment to justify themselves cannot exhibit the graciousness of the cross.

The argument condemns judgment in order to set off the graciousness of the cross, but we deprive the cross of its graciousness by clinging to the argument for its own sake. We use the argument to justify our concept of "grace" at the expense of those who are different from ourselves, but then grace is no longer gracious. It becomes a sword.

Having negated the value of work, we attempted to fill the void that resulted with arguments about grace. We said that grace is unmerited favor, but "unmerited favor" is a concept of value. Grace is not a concept. Grace is the love seen on the cross.

He did not consider equality with God as something to be grasped, but willingly emptied himself, taking the form of a servant.

What do we see when we look at him? A man who attempted to justify himself through the sword of judgment? Was his kindness gracious or was it a sword?

On account of his kindness the religious authorities despised him. They knew the letter of the law and were in love with its dividing power— but they did not know the spirit of the law, which is love.

He healed the sick, gave sight to the blind, preached good news to the poor, just as the prophet said. Do these things show graciousness or the power of the sword? Of a Messiah who comes to conquer death, or one who seeks to conquer the world?

The world can be conquered by the sword—but only grace has the power to conquer death; the grace that makes its meaning known through the love of the cross.

I do not do what I want, but I do the very thing that I hate.

This argument annihilates any possibility of boasting. The apostle loves the law that reflects the spirit of life. Every living being is capable of understanding the goodness of the law, which builds up life, because life is the light of men.

But even as he loves and honors the law, he also finds "another law" at work in him that derives its power from his own mortality and bondage to the grave. This mortal law produces a fear of nothingness and an overwhelming desire to gratify the desire of the flesh to build oneself up at the expense of others.

The apostle knows that the spiritual law is good and loves the gracious life that it describes—but even as he attempts to follow this law he finds himself pulled under by the darkness that is his own mortality. "Oh—wretched man that I am!"

With great graciousness he turns the sword of judgment on himself to show why no one should boast. And this sword condemns boasting about faith and what we believe as well as boasting about works.

The sword of the argument condemns boasting about works if the apostle cannot do what he wants to do but does the very thing he hates. This bleak picture of the human condition makes it impossible to justify ourselves through works and condemns boasting.

But the same sword also condemns the boasting of those who glorify "faith" as if it negated works. They claim to have been remade in a new form by using this force of resistance to annihilate works as if they had no value—but the argument condemns this type of boasting because the apostle is still wretched.

He has not annihilated his old self through faith if it is true that he is still unable to do the good that he desires. He still falls short of the glory of God, and it is this attitude of lowliness that makes him more conscious of the sweetness of grace.

Flesh vs. Spirit

The law is "spiritual" because it is summed up in the command to do no harm to one's neighbor, and this command honors life by seeking to preserve it.

Thus any boasting we might do on the basis of the law is condemned by the law itself, first because no mortal has a right to boast about the law if the law is spiritual—if the law reflects life—but also because boasting about the letter of the law breaks the spirit of the law by harming living beings.

No one should boast about his good works—that is the argument through which the apostle seeks to encourage reconciliation. But to cling to the argument as if it were a negation of work is to obscure the spirituality of the law. If the law is spiritual because it preserves life, then there is value in mortal life and value in work. But if there is no value in mortal life, then the law loses its spiritual significance.

My dear friend—this is just what we have done by using the argument to negate works. If there is no value in works that build up mortal life, works of charity as well as the good work of taking up the lowliness and graciousness of the cross, then there is no value in mortal life itself. By negating works we make the law unspiritual.

If our light is the life that we saw in him, then it is not mortal life that is without value; it is "flesh"—this proud, rebellious existence of ours which is sensuous but which also seeks to justify itself by judging others and raising itself up at their expense.

The cross mortified the flesh in order to build up mortal men. Judgment is the argument, but the meaning is graciousness and mercy. And if the cross has value, then the good work of laying down our own lives also has value—the value of preserving life.

To set the mind on the divisiveness of the flesh is death, but to set the mind on the Spirit brings life and joy.

The flesh is opposed to graciousness because of its bondage to the grave—its fear of nothingness, which goads it into showing the world an iron fist.

Man can hardly afford to open up that fist as long as he clings to judgment to justify himself.

But since faith justifies him apart from works—especially faith in the work of the cross, through which the bondage of death was destroyed—he obtains the freedom to choose between the flesh and the gracious Spirit of life.

This choice cannot become clear unless we clearly understand what it is. To that end it was necessary for the apostle to show that no one can justify himself through work. Since the apostle himself cannot obey the law perfectly, any attempt on his part to justify himself through judgment would bring the whole burden of the law down on his head.

He uses the sword of judgment to show us that it is futile to depend upon law and judgment for justification and to condemn our natural desire to boast about ourselves, but the meaning of the argument is that we should let go of judgment and set our minds on the Spirit of reconciliation seen on the cross.

The argument uses judgment to show the futility of our love of judging—but we cannot set our minds on the Spirit and also continue to cling in our minds to the argument and its dividing power. The argument leads us to the cross, but we must take up the cross itself and its graciousness in order to have life.

To choose graciousness is good work, and to lay down judgment and be reconciled is good work, and to remain completely humble and gentle and live a life of love is also good work. All of these things have great value by the measure of life.

Predestination and the Gift

To further condemn boasting, the letter now goes beyond dividing faith from works to point out that if faith is a gift, then those who believe must have been *chosen* to believe. A gift implies a giver, and the receiver of the gift is the beneficiary of his favor.

The purpose of argument is to encourage humility. We have been given a great gift and should be fully mindful of our good fortune. If we understand how truly blessed we are through this gift, then we will not boast. We will desire to be completely humble and gentle, which mindset is necessary to reconciliation.

If faith is a gift that only some receive, then it seems that God has chosen others to be vessels of destruction by withholding this gift. This too is a reason to remain humble—not to triumph over others. It is not because of us or our merits that we have been blessed by this gift. It is entirely on account of the inscrutable will of the giver.

The desolation seen in those who do not have the gift of faith should not make us proud. It should humble us by reminding us of how fortunate we are to have received the gift. Predestination underlines the graciousness of the gift in order to shame us into being gracious to others and giving up our love of boasting.

But then to claim the mantle of predestination for ourselves, as if the gift singled us out for distinction, is to cling to the argument and violate the meaning.

There is no distinction between Jew and Greek.

In the free gift of faith there is no possibility for distinction and no possibility for boasting. There are no differences by which men might glorify themselves if they are all equally fortunate in the gift.

"If you confess with your mouth that Jesus is Lord and believe in your heart that God raised him from the dead, then you will be saved." In the free gift of faith there is no distinction between Jew or Greek, slave or free, male or female. All are perfectly equal.

The fact that all have fallen short of the glory of God lays the groundwork for the unity of the church and living a life of love. This unity is essential because it reflects the Spirit of life. Without it, there can be no peace or joy.

The church cannot become the body of Christ if some members look down on others. There must be perfect harmony and mutual respect among all members of the body, and Christ himself must be the head.

To have the mind of Christ is to be willing to lay down our lives in order to build up the kingdom of life. To have the mind of Christ is to have in mind the cross, the suffering that comes from giving up selfish desires.

The church that has this passionate suffering in mind is a healthy body, feeding on his sacrifice. But it is impossible to feed on his body and blood without taking up his cross and the self-sacrificing love that was seen on the cross.

"We should not think more highly of ourselves than we ought" if it is only by grace that we have been reconciled to God. We should not judge one another in an attempt to make ourselves seem important.

Instead we should love one another with a sincere love, pursuing the perfect unity of those redeemed by blood with the fervent gratitude of a condemned criminal who has been granted a last-minute reprieve.

Do not think of yourselves more highly than you ought;
love must be sincere.

It is not doctrine that exhibits the mind of Christ; it is the unity of the Spirit that makes us one body. If our doctrines divide us, then we have nothing to boast about. We should be ashamed of our dividedness.

Do some men think highly of themselves because they are circumcised—or because they are uncircumcised? Because they believe they have obeyed the law—or because they think they are showing their freedom from the law? Neither circumcision nor uncircumcision has any value apart from the spirit of the law, which is love. Therefore anyone who boasts is in violation of the law.

Do some men think highly of themselves because they observe feast days—or because they recoil at such observances? Neither observance nor non-observance has any value apart from love. Only by being rooted and grounded in love does it become possible to grasp how deep, how broad, how high is the love of God as revealed in Christ—not through our attitude toward feast days.

Do some men think highly of themselves because they value work and believe in the perfectibility of the human spirit—or others because they cling to faith and believe human matters to be beyond reclamation? Neither faith nor works by themselves mean anything. The only thing that matters is faith expressing itself through love.

Faith cannot be separated from work because all men must act and all men show what they believe through their actions. When we see him naked, we must either clothe or not clothe. When we see him hungry, we must either feed or not feed. There is no third choice, and what we choose reveals what we believe.

If we believe that God has been gracious to us, then we should desire to be gracious to others. We should not abuse his graciousness by taking up the sword of judgment to condemn our fellow believers. We should love them as he loved us, not because we were worthy, but because mercy triumphs over judgment.

Do not pass judgment over disputable matters.

Does one man think that there is good in existence? And yet he acknowledges that this good is so corrupted that no real goodness can be found in it without the redemptive work of the cross; that all that is good is a product of grace.

Does another say that existence is devoid of any goodness? And yet he acknowledges that there are vestiges of the goodness of God in creation and believes that sinners can be made into saints by using the wrath of God to purify their minds.

Both agree that man is fallen and in need of redemption. Both agree that the love of the cross is necessary to reconcile men to God. What is it, then, divides them? Their love of judgment and the power it has to make their arguments seem formidable.

Is grace a "supernatural gift of God" or the "unmerited favor of God"? A gift is unmerited, and that which is unmerited is a gracious gift. It is as if two men were attempting to hold a conversation without realizing that a mirror has been interposed between them. The only thing standing in the way is their love of their own notions of value.

One claims that grace is a substance actually implanted in the fallen being to heal and revive, while another claims that it has no correspondence to human existence and is wholly imputed to heal and revive. Implanted, imputed—what is it that divides them? Not grace itself, but the love of judgment.

It is as if the makers of institutional doctrines had taken Solomon literally and decided to divide the baby. Solomon's judgment is gracious if the birth mother is motivated by love. But without love, judgment leads to death and division.

Put no stumbling block in anyone's way.

Arguments about grace are a stumbling block to those who desire graciousness. How can they see the effects of grace in us when we bite and devour one another? And if they do not see grace, then why should they believe us?

One man believes he can eat anything, since everything that God has made is good; another man feels he must eat vegetables and refrain from the flesh of living creatures. Let each be convinced in his own mind; there is no harm in such beliefs or practices. But we cannot have the mind of Christ if we allow our differences to divide us.

One man believes in implanted grace, another that grace is imputed—but both believe in grace; both agree that it is impossible to obtain life without it. Grace is more important than what men think about grace. Let them cling to grace and be reconciled.

The graciousness of grace

God is not gracious because of doctrine. Grace is gracious because of love.

The graciousness of God is the difference between God and the world—but graciousness has nothing to do with the difference between doctrines. That difference is based on judgment, which is not a gracious power.

Men seek to raise themselves up in the world through their doctrines about grace and appoint themselves keepers of the keys to the kingdom. But love is not self-seeking and does not boast. Love is not seen in the dividing power of doctrine. Love is seen in the reconciling power of the cross.

Grace is expansive and larger than human thinking. It is not a narrow concept of value obtained through the dividing power of judgment but an actual value that beautifies human life. Grace is seen in the rainbow; in the willingness to barter with Abraham; in tolerance for Sarah's impertinent laughter.

Grace is seen in Joseph and his treatment of the brothers who sold him into slavery. Grace is seen the manna and the rock that became a spring, things that were unthinkable and types of things to come. Grace is not limitation, which is product of judgment, but possibility. Grace is the way to go beyond judgment and its limitations.

The difference between grace and the world is seen in the father who welcomes back the prodigal son with a feast and with gladness. The world is the brother, crabbed and limited in its thinking because it clings to judgment. Grace is the joyous quality that resists the limitations of judgment.

Grace is the cross. It is inconceivable to intellect and human ways of thinking that God would lay down his life for men. But the cross does not reflect the power of intellect or judgment. The cross reflects the power of divine love, which transcends judgment.

We have the same choice to make as the older brother, my dear friend. We can continue to make ourselves crabbed and unhappy by clinging to the argument and the divisive power of our doctrines about grace. Or we can feast on the graciousness of God.